RALPH VAUGHAN WILLIAMS

RALPH VAUGHAN WILLIAMS
From a photograph taken in 1936 by Walter Stoneman, F.R.P.S.

RALPH VAUGHAN WILLIAMS

A Study by

Hubert Foss

NEW YORK
OXFORD UNIVERSITY PRESS
1950

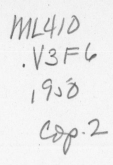

Copyright 1950 by Hubert Foss

Prefatory Note

TOWARDS the writing of these pages many people
have contributed willing aid, and my thanks are warmly
expressed here. First my gratitude goes far out to Ralph
Vaughan Williams himself, who gave me, as a present,
many months ago, the revealing personal account of his own
musical upbringing; he also did me the honour of looking
over the list of works printed at p. 204 *et seq.*, and allowing
me to print his article of 1912. By permission of my
publishers this list of works will be appearing in different
order in the new edition of Grove's *Dictionary of Music and
Musicians*, edited by Eric Blom (to whose help I also pay
tribute). Next there come my friends who read the manuscript in various stages and advised me where to alter
it—Ralph Greaves, Norman Peterkin, Herbert Murrill, and
those who live in my patient family circle. Most of all are
my thanks due to James McKay Martin, without whose
kindly insistence and practical encouragement my pen would
not have flowed. Thanks are due, too, to those who gave me
'hidey-holes' for quiet contemplation and labour—my
friends Sinclair and Edith Logan, near Worcester: my
sister Juliet Rose Foss, at Polegate, Sussex: and Mr and Mrs
Duncan McKenzie, at Cole Green, Herts.

To none of those helpers whose names I have mentioned
—least of them, to the composer, who has resolutely and
rightly taken the fatherly view that he would not read my
manuscript, but confine his help to his valuable contribu-
tions—to none, I repeat, is to be attributed anything but
what few virtues my book may possess. The opinions, the

5

comments, the balances and judgements, expressed therein are mine alone: if any of us differed I had the sole responsibility of decision and of writing the words.

I register here my hearty thanks for all their help, and also to the Royal College of Music, for permission to reprint the essay written for the *R.C.M. Magazine* by the composer himself.

LONDON   H.F.
June 1949

CONTENTS

The musical composer is the most detached of artists. For him the time is either out of joint or irrelevant

DONALD FRANCIS TOVEY,
"The Main Stream of Music,"
in *Essays and Lectures*, 1949.

I

Prologue

THE following pages attempt a study of a great man's mind. They seek his thought through his music, his music through his thought.

When on October 12, 1942, Ralph Vaughan Williams, O.M., reached his seventieth birthday, the British Broadcasting Corporation, directed musically then by Mr Arthur Bliss, did me the honour to invite me to speak in the public arena of the microphone about the man and his music.

The years have passed since then, but I am decided on printing here some of that oral greeting: many years will pass, or I shall myself be a buried cipher, before I would recant a single phrase. Here are the words I spoke on that seventieth birthday—many of them, I feel sure, expanded in what I have later written:

It is not our English custom to utter public praise about our living composers and writers without some outward prompting. Rather, in Milton's words, we "on occasion's forelock watchful wait." Our habit is tardily, even reluctantly, to assimilate their music, but to postpone the moment of its final criticism.

Occasion has now come—for myself a long-looked-for occasion—to pay public tribute to one of our great men. Ralph Vaughan Williams, a composer, attained the age of seventy on Monday last, October 12, and during this week honour is done to him, and pleasure given to all of us, by the British Broadcasting Corporation, for they are playing to us his music on each one of these seven days.

This occasion—honourable, even picturesque, though it

is—I submit is of no great or momentous importance, save for one point: the point is this—it marks the *second* thirty-five years of a life devoted to composing music. By the age of thirty Mozart, Schubert, our own Purcell, had attained the height of their powers as we know them. The new voice in English music, which is Vaughan Williams's voice, was not heard until he was thirty-five. These succeeding thirty-five years have been one long process of development —the latter half of his life has been a successive and successful search after musical truth. An unusual situation occurs—musical critics who did not like his music of twenty-odd years ago have got to admit to-day they were judging Vaughan Williams on insufficient evidence. They had not heard the real music.

So, I tell you, we celebrate this week, not the attainment of a fine old age, but the astonishing spectacle of a composer growing younger, fresher, stronger with each work he writes—a composer who has but lately entered a new field, the field of film music—a composer who has—it is no secret now—another great work up his sleeve with which (as if he were thirty-five years younger) he is still not satisfied.[1]

The musical scene in England in 1907 was indeed such as to make one think of an earlier cry—Wordsworth's sonnet beginning "Milton, thou shouldst be living in this hour." In our English music a Miltonic figure appeared, offering us the *Sea Symphony* in his hands; the epic scale is already visible here, and also in the songs called *On Wenlock Edge*, and here too is the same fighting love of truth that can be found in Milton's *Areopagitica*. Milton's landscape is essentially English, and behind Vaughan Williams's music I can always see, like the little Italian landscapes behind the figures in the early Italian paintings, a view of the English countryside. This music has, just as Milton had, a strong feeling for the English language—its flexibilities, its obstinacy—so like our national character. But I would suggest that Vaughan Williams is far more particular than Milton

[1] The D major Symphony.

in his images. His London is actual, his pastoral scene the living fields. There is no smell of midnight oil, no artificial polish. Vaughan Williams attaches his music to realities— to the songs of the people, the Welshman's hymns, the sound of a brass band in the street or a Church choir in the chancel.

I think, while I am talking, of William Blake. In Vaughan Williams you will find the widely imaginative, almost wild drawings of Blake's designs, and Blake's Biblical imagery, Blake's quick poetry and remote mysticism.

Let us look again. Not only in the operas of Vaughan Williams does one find the dramatic range of Shakespeare. In the *London Symphony* and in *Five Tudor Portraits* come Shakespeare's close touch with humanity, his understanding sympathy with us all, his kindly but incisive humour.

Another comparison—Thomas Hardy. The symphonic style of Vaughan Williams approximates closely to Hardy's method of writing. Neither will dogmatize: both seek a new and particular truth each time. Note how in both these poets and thinkers human details give way to philosophic truths as they progress and develop: *The Dynasts*, the F minor Symphony, both have a sense of splendour without tinsel.

Milton and Shakespeare—Blake and Hardy—these are great names in our English heritage. I have not the least hesitation, nor the least fear of contradiction, in placing the name of Ralph Vaughan Williams alongside them. Here, in our midst, composing music: composing—I press the point—magnificently: here is a great Englishman, living simply, doing his war work like any (I hope all) of us. I have chosen poets for comparison rather than musicians, because our English poetry is supreme in world history beyond denial. Our English music stopped short too soon. The splendid fame and achievement of our Elizabethan composers—Tallis and Byrd, Gibbons, Weelkes, and Wilbye —Vaughan Williams bids fair to bring back their Golden Age to us. He stands in equal eminence with every great name I have mentioned. Let us hear him with respect and with enjoyment.

2

Biographical Details

"SWITZERLAND," wrote Philip Guedalla in one of his better epigrams—"Switzerland to the uninformed observer must always seem to be one of those fortunate countries (the United States are another) which have a great deal of geography and very little history." Of Ralph Vaughan Williams one might say, in parallel, that he has a great deal of music and very little biography. Anecdotes, personal reminiscences, adoring tributes, the composer himself detests. It is fundamental in him. He wrote in a letter to me, "Keep the biographical as small as possible."

Mr Ernest Newman successfully crested the swollen seas of Wagnerean literature with a biography which relates life to works. On the other hand, in Grove's *Dictionary* M. D. Calvocoressi writes of Maurice Ravel, "From that time [1905] onwards, the only landmarks in his biography are the dates of composition and performance of his works." And, in similar terms, Fuller-Maitland writes of Brahms in *Grove:* "Probably there was never a career less eventful than his." A wise writer has said, "A musician's work is, more than that of most artists, far more important than the events of his life." Seeking stronger precedent, I found in the *Dictionary of National Biography*, Supplement 1922–30, the article written by Vaughan Williams himself on Cecil Sharp, in which biography is confined to a few preliminary lines, while his work is allowed to occupy the rest of the entry. I cannot do better than follow my subject's own precept and example, with the enormous added advantage that he has written for this book a chapter of musical autobiography, which is printed here immediately to follow, and to clothe with flesh this slight skeleton of dates and places.

Ralph Vaughan Williams, born on October 12, 1872, the son of the Rev. Arthur Vaughan Williams, Rector of Down Ampney, Gloucestershire, comes, despite his Welsh name, from that Western English county which has given our music Hadow, Holst, Howells, Gurney, and others. His family has legal traditions, at least three judges having borne the name, and is intermingled with that of the Wedgwoods, the famous potters.

Entering Charterhouse in 1887, Ralph Vaughan Williams proceeded thence in 1890 to the Royal College of Music, to study composition under Hubert Parry and (later) Charles Stanford and organ under Walter Parratt. His compositions, writes H. C. Colles in *Grove*, "certainly made less mark than those of his contemporaries"—Coleridge-Taylor, Hurlstone, Holst, among others. At the end of two years he moved to Trinity College, Cambridge, where during his three years of residence he continued his organ lessons with Alan Gray (organist of Trinity) and his composition study with Charles Wood (later Professor of Music in the University of Cambridge). Vaughan Williams took his graduate's degree of Bachelor of Music in 1894 and his Arts bachelorship in 1895. After that he returned to the Royal College of Music for another spell, and at or about the same moment became organist of South Lambeth Church.

But certain important things were happening to him during this academic period. In 1890 a visit to Munich, and another in 1896 to Bayreuth, introduced him to Wagner at first hand. He also went to the Akademie der Kunst in Berlin, studying there under Max Bruch. At home he gave some university extension lectures. Paris, too, came within his orbit. No immediate need to earn his living as a paid musician pressed upon him; but it should be added that music has never allowed Vaughan Williams any of the leisure of idleness.

The next ten years show some remarkable compositions,

certain of which (*Silent Noon, Linden Lea*, and some of the *Songs of Travel* are the obvious examples) constitute even to-day a main connecting line between the mind of the great composer and the great public. We find Vaughan Williams taking his Cambridge Doctorate of Music in 1901, and in 1904 joining the new English Folk-song Society. But he had found English native song (in 1903 or earlier) before he joined the central body, and by 1905 was collecting folk-songs, at King's Lynn, in Norfolk, like a trained anthro-pologist. In 1904 or so he was called upon by the committee of the *English Hymnal* (as it was to be named)—a committee comprising the late Dr Percy Dearmer and Athelstan Riley —to edit the music for this new hymn-book which was to break down a bad Victorian-Mendelssohnian tradition. The book set out to be a "collection of the best hymns in the English language," "a humble companion to the Book of Common Prayer," offered to "all broad-minded men . . . learned and simple alike." No more fortunate task, from the editors' as well as from our composer's point of view, could have been found for Vaughan Williams at this stage in his slowly unfolding development.

Round about 1908 Vaughan Williams decided, on advice, to take a few lessons from Maurice Ravel; he himself gives some account of them. It should be added that Ravel's French influence was grossly overrated in judgements passed by certain critics on the subsequent music.

A commission from the Purcell Society in 1910 to edit the second volume of the *Welcome Songs* has its place in this career, and so has the article in the *R.C.M. Magazine*, published in 1912; a reprint of it is given as an appendix to this book. The idea for an English opera was already germinating in Vaughan Williams's mind in 1911: he wanted to put a boxing-match on the musical stage, and from 1911 to 1914 he was simmering over the libretto with the late Harold Child (of *The Times* and the *Observer*), than whom few better collaborators for a stage piece in the English tradition could at the time have been chosen.

So we come to *A London Symphony*. Other orchestral and choral works had been composed and played: *In the Fen Country* and the *Norfolk Rhapsodies* (of which one alone is allowed survival), *Toward the Unknown Region* (Leeds Festival, 1907), *A Sea Symphony* (Leeds Festival, 1910), *On Wenlock Edge* (for tenor voice and piano quintet, 1909), the *Fantasia on a Theme by Thomas Tallis* (Gloucester, 1910), the *Five Mystical Songs* (Worcester, 1911), the *Fantasia on Christmas Carols* (Hereford, 1912), the music to Aristophanes's *Wasps* (Cambridge, 1908), and some songs already mentioned. The English public, even more tardy then than now to recognize their own countrymen's talents, had hardly discovered this new voice. *A London Symphony* was needed, and came at a good moment psychologically: it was a work of big appeal, commanding wide sympathies. First played in March 1914, with the late Geoffrey Toye conducting at a concert given by the late F. B. Ellis, it looked to have a fair chance. Then came Serajevo, and the outburst of that German spirit of domination over Europe first, and then over the whole civilized world, for which we had to fight a more than thirty years' war.

Vaughan Williams enlisted as an orderly in the R.A.M.C., landing eventually in Macedonia. A more combatant stage of war activity began with his being commissioned in 1917, after a heavy-gunnery course, in the Royal Garrison Artillery, in which regiment he served in France (1917–18) as a lieutenant. The revised version of the *London Symphony* was played under Adrian Boult at the Queen's Hall in January 1918, the composer present, with air-raid warnings and police-whistles sounding.

Immediately after the First World War Vaughan Williams became a Professor of Composition at the Royal College of Music, and many composers of later distinction passed through his hands. The Leith Hill Musical Festival, founded in March 1905 for the villagers of Surrey and the neighbourhood to meet for music-making in Dorking once a year, has been conducted by Vaughan Williams since its inception. The year 1920 saw him as conductor of the (London) Bach Choir, a post he held till 1926; during that holding he learnt much about practical musicianship which his own natural inabilities as a performer had before denied to him. Some of the elements he had learnt at South Lambeth Church.

An honorary Doctorate of Music (Oxon) was awarded to Vaughan Williams in 1919. The *Four Hymns* are dated, for publication, 1920. The year 1922 gave us the *Pastoral Symphony*, the same year that also produced Bax's First and Bliss's "Colour" Symphonies. A new path was taken in the Mass in G minor, which the late Sir Richard Terry performed at Westminster Cathedral in 1923. That same year there came a visit to the United States of America, and the Norfolk Festival in Connecticut. His public operatic career starts from 1922, with a rehearsal performance of *The Shepherds of the Delectable Mountains* at the R.C.M., followed by *Hugh the Drover* in 1924. Another American visit occurs in 1932, for a course of lectures (now made into a book called *National Music*) at Bryn Mawr College, Pennsylvania. Since Cecil Sharp's death in 1933 Vaughan Williams has directed the music for the English Folk-song and Dance Society. In 1934 he was given an honorary life-fellowship of the Worshipful Company of Musicians, and in 1935, having refused (it is no secret) earlier offers of honours, he accepted the great distinction of the Order of Merit.

The Second World War did not seem to afford an outlet for his willing labours except on a salvage-cart not wholly suited to such a composer, and as an addresser of envelopes —an occupation even less suited to one of such individual handwriting!

Two particular tasks (apart from an occasional piece of ceremonial music) later came his way which were more fitting and absorbing—the chairmanship of the Home Office Voluntary Committee to advise on proper releases of alien musicians interned; and the composing of music for propaganda or documentary films.

It may perhaps be added in conclusion that Vaughan Williams is in person a man of big build, of yeoman appearance, countrified by nature and wish, sociable but not social, and uncompromisingly truthful in utterance. His photograph, reproduced as a frontispiece to this book (he has not so far consented to sit for a formal painting), pictures him clearly, and has exactly that merit as a work of art which is the merit of Vaughan Williams's own music—that the more often you look at it, the greater the truth you see in it. In these later years of maturity his conversation has grown noticeably more terse, more witty, and at the same time more beneficent. Always supremely interested in the growth of music rather than in its manufacture, he has consistently been a ready helper of the young musician and the beginning composer, of the unsuccessful or the thwarted musician, of the sick player and the bereaved.

Let these few words, I beg, serve as a humble introduction to the real biography which follows—that which the composer himself has written.

B

3

Musical Autobiography

by Ralph Vaughan Williams

OF the perils of biography Samuel Butler wrote: "It is next to never that we can get at any man's genuine opinion on any subject, except the weather or eating and drinking." Vaughan Williams has written for this book his own account of his early musical life, which is printed in the following pages. They show that the next-to-never chance has fortunately arrived for those who read them; the writer of them has not only the knowledge but the judgment to discern the truth. Vaughan Williams's own words read thus:

My first teacher in musical theory was my aunt, Miss Wedgwood. When I was about six I wrote a pianoforte piece, four bars long, called, heaven knows why, *The Robin's Nest*. It was shown to some musical visitors, and my sister heard one of them say, "Has he learnt any thorough bass?" My sister and I pondered for long over what thorough bass could be. Of course, it never occurred to us to ask. However, soon after this my aunt took me through a book which I still have, called *"The Child's Introduction to Thorough Bass in Conversations of a Fortnight between a Mother and her Daughter aged ten years old* (London, printed for Baldwin Cradock and Joy, 14, Paternoster Row, 1819)." Here is a specimen from Conversation 8:

MARY. Mama, have I anything more to learn about the chord of the seventh?

MOTHER. Yes, you already know how a simple chord of the seventh is formed, but you are also to learn that there are four different kinds of sevenths.

From this I went on to Stainer's *Harmony*, and when I was about eight I went in for a correspondence course organized by Edinburgh University, and, so far as I can remember, passed both the preliminary and advanced examinations. My handwriting was, at that time, considered too bad (I am told that some people still hold this extraordinary opinion),[1] and I was allowed to dictate my exercises to my aunt.

Meanwhile I had been taught the pianoforte, which I never could play, and the violin, which was my musical salvation. I remember as if it were yesterday, when I was about, I think, seven years old, walking with my mother through the streets of Eastbourne and seeing in a music shop an advertisement of violin lessons. My mother said to me, "Would you like to learn the violin?" and I, without thinking, said "Yes." Accordingly next day a wizened old German called Cramer appeared on the scene and gave me my first violin lesson.

I took my violin with me to a preparatory school at Rottingdean, where I had lessons from a well-known Brighton teacher, Quirke. The climax of my career at Rottingdean was when I played Raff's *Cavatina* at a school concert. Fifty years later, at one of the Three Choirs' Festivals, I was suddenly moved to seize W. H. Reed's violin and play through Raff's *Cavatina* by heart, double stops and all, while Reed vamped an accompaniment, before a discerning and enthusiastic audience. But to continue my violin career to its bitter end: at Charterhouse I joined the school orchestra and played second violin, changing later to viola. I also played in Haydn string quartets with Colonel Lewin and his musical family in the holidays, and on Sundays at school I used to go to Mr Girdlestone, one of the masters, where with several other boys we played through Concerti Grossi by the great Italian masters. I owe a great deal to these ensemble experiences.

I remember my first practical lesson in orchestration. The

[1] See p. 16.

school band was playing the slow movement of Beethoven's
First Symphony. The violas were quite close to the one horn
in the orchestra, and my first lesson in orchestral texture
came from hearing the holding note on the horn which
accompanies the reiterated figure of the violas. I believe I
should have made quite a decent fiddler, but the authorities
decided that if I was to take up music at all the violin was
too "doubtful" a career and I must seek safety on the organ
stool—a trade for which I was entirely unsuited; indeed, I
have the distinction of being the only pupil who entirely
baffled Sir Walter Parratt, though I must add, for my own
credit, that later on I passed the F.R.C.O. examination.
Allen always insists that I must have bribed the examiners.

One great landmark in my musical education came while
I was still at my preparatory school at Rottingdean. It was
decided that I was to have some pianoforte lessons from the
visiting teacher, Mr C. T. West. First he gave me the
ordinary music-teacher's rubbish—*Petite Valse* and so on—
but he had the insight to perceive that I should like something better, and one day he brought me a little book which
I have always considered a great treasure—Novello's *Bach
Album*. Bach had never been part of the home curriculum—
Handel, Mozart, Haydn, and some early Beethoven was
what we were fed on at home. My brother, sister, and I were
encouraged to play pianoforte duets from funny old volumes
containing choruses from *Messiah* and *Israel*, which I loved,
and arias from *Don Giovanni* and *Figaro*, which bored me,
though I have to admit that we played the Overture to
Figaro at about ♩ = 50, my aunt complaining that it
was the fashion to play it much too fast.

Later we added Schubert's marches and Haydn's symphonies to our repertoire. Since those early times I have
never wavered in my admiration of Haydn. I remember one
episode which disturbed me in my study of him. My aunt
disapproved of waltzes and thought they were vulgar. Now,
the second subject of Haydn's "Symphony" is undoubtedly
a waltz. Haydn, I knew, was a great composer; a waltz, I

knew, was something vulgar. Surely a great composer could not write anything vulgar? The problem remained unsolved.

Of Bach I then knew nothing, and I imagined vaguely that he was like Handel but not so good. This Bach album was a revelation, something quite different from anything I knew, and Bach still remains for me in a niche by himself.

One episode in my career at Charterhouse must be told. I had the temerity to approach Dr Haig-Brown, the headmaster (and headmasters were headmasters in those days, not the hail-fellow-well-met-young-feller-me-lads of modern times), to obtain the loan of the school hall to give a concert of compositions by myself and a school friend, H. Vivian Hamilton, who afterwards became well known as a pianist. My chief contribution to the programme was a pianoforte trio in one movement. All I remember about it is that the principal theme was distinctly reminiscent of César Franck, a composer whose name I did not even know in those days, and whom I have since learned to dislike cordially. I must have got the theme from one of the French or Belgian imitators of Franck whose salon music was popular in those days. I remember that after the concert James Noon, the mathematical master, came up to me and said in that sepulchral voice which Carthusians of my day knew so well, "Very good, Williams, you must go on." I treasured this as one of the few words of encouragement I ever received in my life!

On leaving Charterhouse in 1890 I went direct to the Royal College of Music, but during the intervening summer holidays one very important thing happened. I went to Munich and heard my first Wagner opera. We found that *Die Walküre* was down for that evening. The opera, we were told, would start at seven, so at six o'clock we sat down to have a preliminary meal. Hardly had we started when the waiter rushed in—he had made a mistake—on a Wagner *Abend* the Opera started at six. The rest decided for dinner, but I, like the hero of a novel, "left my food untasted" and

rushed off to the Opera House. I arrived just in time to hear
that wonderful passage for strings when Sieglinde offers
Siegmund the cup. This was my first introduction to later
Wagner, but I experienced no surprise, but rather that
strange certainty that I had heard it all before. There was a
feeling of recognition as of meeting an old friend which comes
to us all in the face of great artistic experiences. I had the
same experience when I first heard an English folk-song,
when I first saw Michelangelo's *Day and Night*, when I
suddenly came upon Stonehenge or had my first sight of
New York City—the intuition that I had been there already.

That September I entered as a student at the R.C.M., and
was determined if possible to study composition under
Parry. I had first heard of Parry some years before, when
I was still a schoolboy. I remember my cousin, Stephen
Massingberd, coming into the room full of that new book
Studies of Great Composers.[1] "This man Parry," he said,
"declares that a composer must write music as his musical
conscience demands." This was quite a new idea to me, the
loyalty of the artist to his art. Soon after that I got to know
some of his music, especially parts of *Judith*, and I remember
even as a boy saying to my brother that there was something,
to my mind, peculiarly English about his music. So I was
quite prepared to join with the other young students of the
R.C.M. in worshipping at that shrine, and I think I can
truly say that I have never been disloyal to it. Perhaps I can
no longer, owing to the weakening digestion of old age,
swallow Parry's music whole, as I did then; but I still thrill
to the magnificence of *Job* and *De Profundis*, and I hereby
solemnly declare, keeping steadily in view the works of
Byrd, Purcell, and Elgar, that *Blest Pair of Sirens* is my
favourite piece of music written by an Englishman.

By a wise ruling of the College, which I fear no longer
obtains, no one was allowed to study composition until he
had passed Grade 5 in harmony. So for two terms I did my
theoretical work with Dr F. E. Gladstone. Under his

[1] Published in 1887.

guidance I worked through every exercise in Macfarren's *Harmony*, a discipline for which I have ever since been grateful.

After two terms I passed my Grade 5 harmony and was allowed to become a pupil of Parry. I will not try to describe what this experience meant to a boy. I was very elementary at the time. I blush with shame now when I think of the horrible little songs and anthems which I presented for his criticism. Parry's great watchword was "characteristic." He was always trying to discover the character revealed in even the weakest of his students' compositions.

Before telling the following story I ought to explain that Parry, not content with the official lesson, used to keep his pupils' compositions to look at during the week. One day, through pure carelessness, I had written out a scale passage with one note repeated and then a gap. Parry said, "I have been looking at this passage for a long time to discover whether it is just a mistake or whether you meant anything characteristic."

I was painfully illiterate in those days, even more so than now. Parry could hardly believe that I knew so little music. One day he was talking to me about the wonderful climax in the development of the *Appassionata* Sonata. Suddenly he realized that I did not know it, so he sat down at the pianoforte and played it through to me. There were showers of wrong notes, but in spite of that it was the finest performance that I have heard. So I was told to study more Beethoven, especially the posthumous quartets, "as a religious exercise." At that time I hated Beethoven. I was suffering from an overdose of Gounod, and I could not understand why the tune in the finale of the *Eroica* Symphony was good music, while the "Judex" from *Mors et Vita* was bad music. (I was only eighteen, please, teacher!) To this day the Beethoven idiom repels me, but I hope I have at last learnt to see the greatness that lies behind the idiom that I dislike, and at the same time to see an occasional weakness behind the Bach idiom which I love.

Parry was very generous in lending scores to his pupils. (This was long before the days of miniature scores and gramophone records.) I borrowed *Siegfried* and *Tristan* and Brahms's *Requiem*, and for some time after my so-called compositions consisted entirely of variations of a passage near the beginning of that work.

I remember one day when I came in for my lesson I found a fellow-student, Richard Walthew, borrowing the score of the Prelude to *Parsifal*. Parry condemned it as the weakest of the Wagner preludes—"mere scene-painting" was, I think, his description of it. He was always very insistent on the importance of form as opposed to colour. He had an almost moral abhorrence of mere luscious sound. It has been said that Parry's own orchestration was bad; the truth is, I think, that he occasionally went too far in his deliberate eschewal of mere orchestral effect. Years after this I was sitting next to Elgar at a rehearsal of Parry's *Symphonic Variations*, with its curious spiky sound. I said, "I suppose many people would call this bad orchestration; I do not find it so." Elgar turned on me almost fiercely: "Of course it's not bad orchestration; the music could have been scored in no other way."

Parry's criticism was constructive. He was not merely content to point out faults, but would prescribe the remedy. The last two bars of my early song, "The Willow Song," were almost certainly composed by Parry.

Parry once said to me, "Write choral music as befits an Englishman and a democrat." We pupils of Parry have, if we have been wise, inherited from Parry the great English choral tradition which Tallis passed on to Byrd, Byrd to Gibbons, Gibbons to Purcell, Purcell to Battishill and Greene, and they in their turn through the Wesleys to Parry. He has passed on the torch to us, and it is our duty to keep it alight.

I have already mentioned Richard Walthew. We became great friends, and, though we hardly ever meet now, I hope the friendship still subsists. This, however, is a record not of friendships, but of musical influences, and I pick out Walthew's name among friends of that period because I learnt much from him. I used occasionally to go to his house at Highbury and play duets with him—or, rather, he played and I stumbled behind him as best I could. In this way I learnt to know a lot of music, including, I remember, Stanford's *Irish Symphony*. In those days, before the gramophone and the wireless and the miniature score, the pianoforte duet was the only way, unless you were an orchestral player, of getting to know orchestral music, and only really got to know it from the inside; not in the superficial way of lazily listening to a gramophone record. One day Walthew, who had a holy horror of anything high-falutin' in art, insisted on taking me to hear *Carmen*. By that time I had quite recovered from my Gounod fever and had become the complete prig. Bach, Beethoven (*ex officio*), Brahms, and Wagner were the only composers worth considering, so I went to *Carmen* prepared to scoff; but Walthew won the day and I remained to pray. It must have been about the same time that I had another salutary disturbance of my musical prejudices: I heard Verdi's *Requiem* for the first time. At first I was properly shocked by the frank sentimentalism and sensationalism of the music. I remember being particularly horrified at the drop of a semitone on the word 'Dona.' Was not this the purest 'village organist'? But in a very few minutes the music possessed me. I realized that here was a composer who could do all the things which I, with my youthful pedantry, thought wrong—indeed, would be unbearable in a lesser man; music which was sentimental, theatrical, occasionally even cheap, and yet was an overpowering masterpiece. That day I learnt that there is nothing in itself that is "common or unclean"; indeed, that there are no canons of art except that contained in the well-worn tag, "To thine own self be true."

In 1892 I went to Cambridge, where I had lessons from Charles Wood in preparation for the Mus. Bac. degree. Charles Wood was the finest technical instructor I have ever known. I do not say necessarily the greatest teacher. I do not think he had the gift of inspiring enthusiasm or of leading to the higher planes of musical thought. Indeed, he was rather prone to laugh at artistic ideals, and would lead one to suppose that composing music was a trick anyone might learn if he took the trouble. But for the craft of composition he was unrivalled, and he managed to teach me enough to pull me through my Mus. Bac. I also had organ lessons from Alan Gray. Our friendship survived his despair at my playing, and I became quite expert at managing the stops at his voluntaries and organ recitals.

In the year 1892 there also came to Cambridge as organ scholar an undergraduate rather older than the rest—H. P. Allen. I believe I had the honour of first introducing him to the music of Brahms. Allen at once took over the Amateur University Musical Club, shook them out of their complacency, and made them rehearse such things as the Schumann and Brahms Pianoforte Quintets and Schubert's String Quintet. I got much musical instruction in listening to the rehearsal of these works, which I came to know nearly by heart. Allen also gave me an opportunity of hearing, for the first time, a semi-public performance of a composition of my own—a quartet for men's voices. At the first performance the second tenor got a bar out, and remained so nearly to the end. Allen organized an encore, and it was done all over again, this time correctly. The audience disliked it the second time even more than the first. This may seem a small episode, but it was my first experience of an essential and salutary, though unpleasant, form of composition lesson—a performance in public, something quite different from a private rehearsal.

Allen did me the same service, though on a larger scale, in 1910, when, after my *Sea Symphony* had had a very doubtful reception at the Leeds Festival, he at once arranged for performances at Oxford and in London, though he confessed to me afterwards that he had had grave doubts himself as to its artistic success.

While I was at Cambridge I conducted a small choral society, which met on Sundays to sing Schubert's Masses. If a composer cannot play in an orchestra or sing in a choir, the next best thing he can do in self-education is to try his hand at conducting, and really find out what the performers are up against. The only way to learn to conduct is to 'try it on the dog.' This is much better than any amount of class-teaching, about which I have grave doubts. According to Wagner, the duty of the conductor is to give the proper tempo to the orchestra. Elgar said, "When I conduct I let the orchestra play." A good orchestra will play well if the conductor will let them and they play no better because he makes funny faces at them. (It is different with a chorus; they fail to come in altogether if they don't get the right grimace.) The two best conducting lessons I ever had were from my old friend Isidore Schwiller, the violinist, who taught me how to start an orchestra on an up-beat, and from Mr Henderson, the famous timpanist of the L.S.O. of old days, who said to me, "You give us a good square four-in-the-bar and we'll do the rest." To which I may add Stanford's witty saying, "A conductor need never be nervous; he can't make any wrong notes."

After Cambridge I went back to the R.C.M. Parry was, by this time, Director, so I went for lessons to Stanford. Stanford was a great teacher, but I believe I was unteachable. I made the great mistake of trying to fight my teacher. The way to get the best out of instruction is to put oneself entirely in the hands of one's instructor, and try to find out all about his method regardless of one's own personality, keeping, of course, a secret *eppur si muove* up one's sleeve. Young students are much too obsessed with the idea of expressing their personalities. In the merest harmony exercises they insist on keeping all their clumsy progressions because that is what they 'felt,' forgetting that the art cannot mature unless the craft matures alongside with it.

The details of my work annoyed Stanford so much that we seldom got beyond these to the broader issues, and the lesson usually started with a conversation on these lines: "Damnably ugly, my boy. Why do you write such things?" "Because I like them." "But you can't like them, they're not music." "I shouldn't write them if I didn't like them." So the argument went on, and there was no time left for any constructive criticism. Stanford tried—I fear in vain—to lighten my texture. He actually made me write a waltz. I was much bitten by the modes at that time, and I produced a modal waltz! I really must have been unteachable and hopelessly obstinate.

Stanford never displayed great enthusiasm for my work. I once showed him a movement of a quartet which had caused me hours of agony, and I really thought was going to move mountains this time. "All rot, my boy," was his only comment. But his deeds were better than his words— later on he introduced my work to the Leeds Festival, thus giving me my first opportunity of a performance under these imposing conditions. When all is said and done, what one really gets out of lessons with a great man cannot be computed in terms of what he said to you or what you did for him, but in terms of the intangible contact with his mind and character. With Stanford I always felt I was in the presence of a lovable, powerful, and enthralling mind. This helped me more than any amount of technical instruction.

What one really learns from Academy or College is not so much from one's official teachers as from one's fellow-students. I was lucky in my companions in those days. Other students at the college were Dunhill, Ireland, Howard-Jones, Fritz Hart, and Gustav Holst. We used to meet in a little teashop in Kensington and discuss every subject under the sun, from the lowest note of the double bassoon to the philosophy of *Jude the Obscure*. I learnt more from these conversations than from any amount of formal teaching, but I felt at a certain disadvantage with these companions: they were all so competent and I felt such an amateur. I have struggled all my life to conquer amateurish technique, and, now that perhaps I have mastered it, it seems too late to make

any use of it. Curiously, however, as regards orchestral
texture, when I hear my early works, written when my
knowledge was still all out of books and I had to sit for an
hour wondering what to do with the 2nd clarinet in a loud
tutti, my orchestration seems fuller and richer than nowadays,
when my writing is backed by practical experience. And
here I should like to mention the names of two men who
have helped me in my orchestral work—Cecil Forsyth,
before he went to America, 'vetted' many of my scores,
giving out from his incomparable store of knowledge,
obtained 'straight from the horse's nosebag.' Gordon Jacob
is the other name. He was, at one time, nominally my pupil,
though there was nothing I could teach him, at all events in
the matter of technique, which he did not know better than
I. Since then I have often asked his advice on points of
orchestration, as, indeed, I would gladly do in any branch
of the composer's art.

In 1895 I was appointed to my first and last organ post—
St Barnabas, South Lambeth. As I have already said, I
never could play the organ, but this appointment gave me
an insight into good and bad Church music which stood me
in good stead later on. I also had to train the choir, and
give organ recitals, and accompany the services, which gave
me some knowledge of music from the performer's point of
view. I also founded a choral society and an orchestral
society, both of them pretty bad, but we managed once to do
a Bach Cantata, and I obtained some of that practical
knowledge of music which is so essential to a composer's
make-up. Composers who think that they will achieve their
aim by ranging apart and living the life beautiful make the
great mistake of their lives. Wagner could never have
written *Tristan* and *Meistersinger* if he had not had those years
of gruelling experience at Dresden. Brahms ought certainly
to have accepted that Kapellmeistership in that small
German town whose name I forget.[1] Intimate acquaintance
with the executive side of music in orchestra, chorus, and

First at Cologne, and later, more importantly, at Hamburg.

opera made even Mahler into a very tolerable imitation of a composer.

In 1897 I decided to have a few months' study and experience abroad. Stanford wanted me to go to Italy and hear opera at the Scala. He thought I was too Teuton already. He did not want me to take definite lessons with anyone. But I disregarded his advice and went to Berlin. My reason for this choice, I believe, was the extraordinary one that Berlin was the only town at that time where they performed *The Ring* without cuts! I had an introduction to Herzogenberg, who looked at my work and said it reminded him of Mascagni, and advised me to study with Max Bruch. It is difficult to say what it is one learns from a teacher. I only know that I worked hard and enthusiastically, and that Max Bruch encouraged me, and I had never had much encouragement before. With my own pupils now I always try to remember the value of encouragement. Sometimes a callow youth appears who may be a fool or may be a genius, and I would rather be guilty of encouraging a fool than of discouraging a genius. A fool, after all, may find his own salvation in artistic self-expression, even though it means nothing to anyone else, and as to the genius, perhaps one may by analogy quote Lord Chesterfield—"If it's fine take an umbrella; if it's raining, please yourself."

When I was under Stanford I used to vex him much with my flattened sevenths. He tried to prove to me that the flat leading note was pure theory, and that all folk-songs descended on to the tonic; but I felt in my bones that he was wrong, though it was only later, when I heard traditional singers, that I was able to prove my point to my own satisfaction. Max Bruch was equally worried by this idiosyncrasy of mine: he said, "*Sie haben eine Leidenschaft für die Kleine Septime.*" He also warned me against writing *Augen-musik* as opposed to *Ohren-musik*. This warning was wasted on me, as I habitually and unashamedly use the pianoforte when composing. (I suppose this would be considered part of my amateurishness.) I believe that other composers have done so, though, as R. O. Morris says, "It is always considered as not quite 'playing the game.'" The only two composers, as far as I know, who never used an instrument when composing were Berlioz and Rheinberger. Comment is unnecessary. I heard all the music I could when I was in Berlin, especially operas. Among them were Lortzing's *Undine* and Meyerbeer's *Robert le Diable*. I also remember beautiful performances of Bach Cantatas at the Sing-Akademie. The Joachim and Halir Quartets were at their zenith, and there was a memorable performance at the Hochschule of the Brahms Double Concerto played as a pianoforte trio by Joachim, Hausman, and Barth.

When I came back to London I soon left my organist post and settled down to try and learn how to compose—not by studying, but by doing. However, I still felt the need of instruction, and in about the year 1900 I took my courage in both hands and wrote to Elgar asking him to give me lessons, especially in orchestration. I received a polite reply from Lady Elgar, saying that Sir Edward was too busy to give me lessons, but suggesting that I should become a pupil of Professor Bantock. I did not adopt his suggestion, which was perhaps a mistake, as what Bantock did not know about the orchestra is not worth knowing. But though Elgar would not teach me personally he could not help teaching me through his music. I spent several hours at the British Museum studying the full scores of the *Enigma Variations* and *Gerontius*. The results are obvious in the opening pages of the finale of my *Sea Symphony*, and I have discovered lately that I owe a good deal in this work to an early work of Holst's, *The Mystic Trumpeter*. Holst used also to say that he cribbed from me, though I never perceived it. I do not think that composers ever know when they are being cribbed from. Cribbing is, to my mind, a legitimate and praiseworthy practice, but one ought to know where one has cribbed from. I expect Schubert knew that he cribbed *Death and the Maiden* from Beethoven's Seventh Symphony, but I doubt whether Wagner realized that he had cribbed the *Nibelungen* theme from Schubert's D minor Quartet and the *Rhine* theme from Mendelssohn's *Melusine*.

Deliberate cribbing is all right, and the funny thing is that what is most deliberately cribbed sounds the most original; but the more subtle, unconscious cribbing is, I admit, dangerous. I was quite unconscious that I had cribbed from *La Mer* in the introduction to my *London Symphony* until Constant Lambert horrified me by calling my attention to it.

A strange episode occurred about this time which, though it had no direct bearing on my musical education, must be related here. I burst in on the privacy of Delius (who happened to be in London at the time) and insisted on playing through the whole of my *Sea Symphony* to him. Poor fellow! How he must have hated it! But he was very courteous, and contented himself with saying, "Vraiment, il n'est pas mesquin."

In 1900 I first met Cecil Sharp. He had not then shaken musical England with *Folk-songs from Somerset*. Indeed, I did not imbibe folk-song from Sharp, and when I first started collecting, in 1903, and began boring my friends with them, I left Sharp out of the list because I thought he would not be interested.

I must have made my first contact with English folk-songs when I was a boy in the 'eighties, through Stainer and Bramley's *Christmas Carols, New and Old*. I remember clearly my reaction to the tune of the "Cherry-tree Carol," which was more than simple admiration for a fine tune, though I did not then naturally realize the implications involved in that sense of intimacy. This sense came upon me more strongly in 1893 when I first discovered "Dives and Lazarus" in *English County Songs*. Here, as before with Wagner, I had that sense of recognition—"here's something which I have known all my life—only I didn't know it!"

There has been a lot of cheap wit expended on folk-song composers. The matter seems to boil down to two accusations:

(1) That it is 'cheating' to make use of folk-song material. This is really nothing more than the old complaint of the vested interests who are annoyed when anyone drinks a glass of pure water which he can get free, rather than a glass of beer which will bring profit to the company. This appears to involve a moral rather than an artistic question; from the point of view of musical excellence it seems to me that so long as good music is made it matters very little how it is made or who makes it. If a composer can, by tapping the sources hidden in folk-song, make beautiful music, he will be disloyal to his art if he does not make full use of such an avenue of beauty.

(2) The second accusation is made by people who affect to scorn what is 'folky' because it does not come within the ken of their airless snuggeries, because it does not require any highly paid teachers to inculcate it or the purchase of text-books with a corresponding royalty to the author. It is really a case of the vested interest once again.

Why should music be 'original'? The object of art is to stretch out to the ultimate realities through the medium of beauty. The duty of the composer is to find the *mot juste*. It does not matter if this word has been said a thousand times before, as long as it is the right thing to say at that moment. If it is *not* the right thing to say, however unheard of it may be, it is of no artistic value. Music which is unoriginal is so, not simply because it has been said before, but because the composer has not taken the trouble to make sure that this was the right thing to say at the right moment.

I have never had any conscience about cribbing.

I cribbed Satan's dance in *Job* deliberately from the Scherzo of Beethoven's last Quartet, the opening of my F minor Symphony deliberately from the finale of the Ninth Symphony, and the last two bars of the Scherzo to my *Sea Symphony* from the Mass in D. (I expect that Beethoven knew that he was cribbing the last movement of the *Appassionata* Sonata from one of Cramer's pianoforte studies.) It is said that once when Wagner was rehearsing

C

Meistersinger he stopped in the middle of that rather common-place theme in the Third Act and said, "Gentlemen, does not that come out of the *Merry Wives*?"

My intercourse with Cecil Sharp crystallized and confirmed what I already vaguely felt about folk-song and its relationship to the composer's art. With Sharp it was a case of "Under which king, Bezonian? Speak, or die." You had to be either pro-folk-song or anti-folk-song, and I came down heavily on the folk-song side.

In 1904 I undertook to edit the music of a hymn-book. This meant two years with no 'original' work except a few hymn-tunes. I wondered then if I was 'wasting my time.' The years were passing and I was adding nothing to the sum of musical invention. But I know now that two years of close association with some of the best (as well as some of the worst) tunes in the world was a better musical education than any amount of sonatas and fugues.

As I have already said, I have always found it difficult to study. I have learnt almost entirely what I have learnt by trying it on the dog. Gustav Holst once said to me years ago, "We ought to be writing now what will enable us to write well later on." This was a precept I found very difficult to observe. Young composers are apt to think that what they have written is what the world has been waiting for come at last. This is an intelligible and healthy state of mind, but they are also apt to think that it is 'now or never,' and that this is the last as well as the greatest work they are going to write; and it is this attitude of mind which prevents so many students from learning to compose.

In 1908 I came to the conclusion that I was lumpy and stodgy, had come to a dead-end, and that a little French polish would be of use to me. So I went to Paris armed with an introduction to Maurice Ravel. He was much puzzled at our first interview. When I had shown him some of my work he said that, for my first lesson, I had better "*écrire un petit menuet dans le style de Mozart*." I saw at once that it was time to act promptly, so I said in my best French, "Look here, I have given up my time, my work, my friends, and my career to come here and learn from you, and I am *not* going to write a *petit menuet dans le style de Mozart.*" After that we became great friends and I learnt much from him. For example, that the heavy contrapuntal Teutonic manner was not necessary. "*Complexe, mais pas compliqué*" was his motto. He showed me how to orchestrate in points of colour rather than in lines. It was an invigorating experience to find all artistic problems looked at from what was to me an entirely new angle.

Brahms and Tchaikovsky he lumped together as "*tout les deux un peu lourds*"; Elgar was "*tout à fait Mendelssohn*"; his own music was "*tout à fait simple, rien que Mozart.*" He was against development for its own sake—one should only develop for the sake of arriving at something better. He used to say there was an implied melodic outline in all vital music, and instanced the opening of the C minor Symphony as an example of a tune which was not stated but was implicit. He was horrified that I had no pianoforte in the little hotel where I worked. "*Sans le piano on ne peut pas inventer de nouvelles harmonies.*"

I practised chiefly orchestration with him. I used to score some of his own pianoforte music and bits of Rimsky and Borodin, to whom he introduced me for the first time. After three months I came home with a bad attack of French fever and wrote a string quartet which caused a friend to say that I must have been having tea with Debussy, and a song cycle with several atmospheric effects, but I did *not* succumb to the temptation of writing a piece about a cemetery, and Ravel paid me the compliment of telling me that I was the only pupil who "*n'écrit pas de ma musique.*" The fact is that I could not have written Ravel's music even if I had wanted to. I was quite incapable, even with the piano, of inventing his *nouvelles harmonies.* I sometimes wish that I could think of the strange chords of my old friend Arnold Bax. I hope I am not like the fox without the tail, but I usually feel content to provide good plain cooking, and hope that the proof of the pudding will be in the eating.

My French fever soon subsided, and left my musical metabolism on the whole healthier.

Another potent musical influence was S. P. Waddington. His is one of the best-informed minds on all subjects that I have ever met—one of those people in the presence of whom it is impossible to be mean or petty. He never would give me formal lessons, but he often looked at my work and pronounced sound judgements on it. He was the finest sight-reader I ever met, and, as I could not play at all myself, his playing was often the first occasion I really heard my work. His power of deciphering a manuscript score was almost uncanny. If the manuscript was too illegible he would guess, and invariably guessed right. With this power of sight-reading went that of immediately spotting weak moments and redundant bars. He was a severe critic. "You try to run before you can walk," he once said to me. This was perfectly true; I had not sufficient patience or application to study. I have learnt by trial and error; I have drawers full of these errors—attempts to run, with a fatal stumble almost every other bar. But one bit of study I did undertake. One summer I retired for a month to a Yorkshire farmhouse with several classical scores and the themes of my own 'compositions.' These themes I proceeded to treat and develop according to my classical models, choosing, of course, themes which more or less corresponded in structure. I found this a wonderful discipline, and I have passed it on to my pupils. (I believe Charles Wood used much the same method.) The difficulty is that if the pupils invent *ad hoc* themes they are so colourless that they are incapable of development, and they steadily refuse to make use of themes that they have already composed as being too sacrosanct for such base purposes. The model I most frequently use is the slow movement of Beethoven's Sonata, op. 2, no. 2. It has so many points of subtle structure and development which only a close bar-by-bar analysis reveals.

It was in the early years of this century that I first met George Butterworth. I think it was I who introduced him to folk-song. This was his salvation; his music up to then had showed great promise, but was much overshadowed by Brahms and Schumann. To him, as to me, the folk-song was not an inhibiting but a liberating influence; it certainly helped Butterworth to realize himself and to cast off the fetters of Teutonism.

If I helped Butterworth, much more did he help me. We were talking together one day when he said in his gruff, abrupt manner, "You know, you ought to write a symphony." I answered, if I remember right, that I never had written a symphony and never intended to. (This was not strictly true, for I had in earlier years sketched three movements of one symphony and the first movement of another, all now happily lost.) I suppose that Butterworth's words stung me, and, anyhow, I looked out some sketches I had made for what, I believe, was going to have been a symphonic poem (!) about London, and decided to throw it into symphonic form. Butterworth assiduously saw me through my trouble, and, when the original full score was lost, helped to make a new one from the band parts.

The greatest influence on my music is one about which I feel I can write least. I remember my first meeting with Gustav Holst in 1895 very vividly. He quoted something from Sheridan's *The Critic*. How soon we started our "Field Days" I cannot remember, but it must have been soon. On these occasions we would devote a whole day, or at least an afternoon, to examining each other's compositions. As I say, these orgies must have started early, and they continued to the end—that is to say, for nearly forty years. I think he showed all he wrote to me, and I nearly all I wrote to him. I say 'nearly all' advisedly, because sometimes I could not face the absolute integrity of his vision, and I hid some of my worst crimes from him. I regret now that I did not face even his disapproval. Without him and Waddington to criticize me I sometimes feel lost: they both had the power and the will to give all they had.

Holst would spend hours bringing his mastery, his keen vision, and his feeling for clear texture to bear on my work, especially in those clumsy places where I was continually getting into holes and could not find the way out. He would not rest till he had found a solution for the problem which not only satisfied him, but one which my obstinacy would accept. This was all the more wonderful because Holst, I know, found it difficult to appreciate the amateurish attitude of mind; his absolute sureness of purpose inclined him to be unsympathetic to the vacillations of human nature. This is why, for example, I never showed him my comic opera, because he never would have been able to understand how I could at the same time consider it trivial and yet want to write it.

I should like to place on record all that he did for me when I wrote *Job*. I should be alarmed to say how many "Field Days" we spent over it. Then he came to all the orchestral rehearsals, including a special journey to Norwich, and finally he insisted on the Camargo Society's performing it. Thus I owe the life of *Job* to Holst, just as I owe the life of the *Sea Symphony* to Stanford and Allen.

I remember after the first orchestral rehearsal of *Job* his almost going on his knees to beg me to cut out some of the percussion with which my inferiority complex had led me to overload the score. Over-scoring has always been one of my vices, and it arises, I am convinced, from the fact that I am not always sure enough of myself and have not the courage of my convictions, and that I must hide my nakedness with an apron of orchestration. Holst's orchestra could be naked and unashamed.

4

Comments on Life and Works

AFTER reading the foregoing pages of memories and tendencies the innocent or uninformed reader might be excused if he were to underrate the scale of the man who wrote them. A sympathetic foreigner, for example, might well be lost in the allusions to Parry and Allen, among others of whom he knows nothing. Remove the English names; he would observe references to Max Bruch and Ravel. Bruch had many undistinguished pupils, Ravel fewer. A much smaller man than Vaughan Williams might describe himself adequately in those same words.

Some assumption, then, must be made of the reader's knowledge of Vaughan Williams's music before the further assumption can be made that the composer's own words are fully understood. But would that first assumption be right? In England there are many who know much about music, not many who know much music. Our repertoire is very limited, our chances for studying sound, instead of theory and history, niggardly. A few works by Handel; fewer still of Purcell; a small fraction of Bach's output; the conventionally played concert-pieces of Haydn, Mozart, Schubert, Brahms, and Wagner; a little more—at this moment of writing—by Beethoven and Tchaikovsky; little of the chamber music of all of them, with the barest modicum, if any, of Palestrina, Lassus, Victoria, Byrd and his fellows, and Schütz.

The English public is gradually discovering Vaughan Williams in his old age, having steadily neglected him during all the earlier years. But how often do we hear the Fourth Symphony, *Flos Campi*, the *Magnificat*, the Shelley songs? Is *Hugh the Drover* often played, or *Sir John in Love*?

Yet, the assumption must be made, it is asserted here, that Vaughan Williams is a composer of great stature and of international importance.

> Why, man, he doth bestride the narrow world
> Like a Colossus; and we petty men
> Walk under his huge legs, and peep about
> To find ourselves dishonourable graves.

The turmoil of two wars and the 'long week-end' of 1918–39 have made vast changes—the change from horse to jet-'plane, that from Lee-Enfield to atom bomb or from piano duet to a radio set in every home. Meteors have appeared in the sky, and have fallen, spent. In his fifty years of active composing of music Vaughan Williams has given us an earth-like structure which stands, which I believe will stand, against tidal changes and idiomatic eddies and currents of popularity, and which "the world's great age" (I do not believe it is more importantly to be "built anew" to-day than it was in Shelley's time) may easily overlook, but will one day rediscover.

Herein, then, we have read a large-scale document—the utterance of a great man, which illuminates his mind to a degree of radiance blinding in proportion to one's knowledge of his music. The simplicity is characteristic of Vaughan Williams. The picture he paints is composite, but he uses no elaboration—nothing, indeed, but the simplest words— to round its shape. He does not attempt literary grace, but he is capable of literary truth. Without polishing a phrase or balancing one sentence against another Vaughan Williams has composed a piece of prose that is so bare in its verity as to be a phenomenon. Primitive, it might be called, but not primitive in the self-conscious sense of the pre-Raphaelites, or of the art galleries' cult for African totems. Here is the outspoken, often poetic, word of the peasant mind. Matter takes precedence over manner. Truth is the object; the writing mind is subservient to that end. In its very absence of carefully wrought, studiedly written literary form the prose has an architectural size.

"Music is above all the art of the humble," Vaughan Williams wrote in his only book, *National Music*. (Turn to his paragraphs (pp. 37–38) about Gustav Holst for the humility of greatness.) "We are laughed at in England for our *bourgeoisie*," his book continues; "personally I am proud to be described as a *bourgeois*." The point is enlarged with Bach:

> I remember a young exquisite saying to me that he didn't like Bach "because he was so *bourgeois*." I am not at all sure that it is not a true criticism, and that that is why Bach appeals especially to me. . . . I believe that every community and every mental state should have its artistic equivalent.

This seeking attitude of mind can be described or brought into focus in other ways. The late A. H. Fox Strangways wrote for the second number of his own journal, *Music and Letters*, in April 1920, an essay with parallel comments. About the *Sea Symphony* he writes:

> We remember the composer going about when it was over, asking friends to tell him what to cut out. The modesty of asking us to look five years ahead of him who is ten years ahead of all of us!

That Vaughan Williams has still that habit of mind is evidenced by his submission of the Fifth and Sixth Symphonies, in piano versions, to musicians and friends before he heard a note of the orchestration. For Strangways continues:

> An ideal—such as music typifies—is not of much use without a firm hold on practical life. . . . The ["London"] Symphony was a valiant attempt to hammer beauty out of ugliness, not to go where beauty was and leave ugliness to take care of itself. The attitude to folk-song is no pose. . . . He has had no theories about it, he has simply practised it.

Later on the writer answers the criticisms that technique is lacking, counterpoint untidy, and so on:

> Those who pronounce such verdicts do not fully understand the task he has set himself to accomplish; they forget how much harder

it is to take the every-day things and make them beautiful, than to borrow beauty ready-made and label it as one's own patent.

If, then, I claim nobility of thought for Vaughan Williams, I do not mean a high-falutin', super-æsthetic, remote, or even polished style of writing. He is no Pater, no Ruskin. His mystical thoughts may soar with Herbert or Bridges, but he himself remains tied to the essential earthiness, the actuality, of our music. The material he prefers is the song of the common man, in Church or at leisure; the practical provision for daily use of a Bach or a Purcell; the simple truth expressed clearly, with it matters not how much struggle, nor with how many evidences left strewn on the ground. His sublime is attained by a climb up a ladder that stands on the soil.

Essentially those autobiographical pages are written by a man who is not a theorist. Walter Bagehot called the English "of all the nations in the world the least a nation of philosophers"; and Donald Tovey, in one of his brilliant asides, once said to me, "Of course, Vaughan Williams is a man of action." That these words were spoken in compliment we can see if we turn to Tovey's Romanes Lecture, *Normality and Freedom in Music*, where he says, "Art is an activity, and our ideas of what is normal to it must not be confused by notions appropriate only to fixed points." "Even Monteverdi experimented first" (the lecture continues later) "and theorized afterwards in self-defence."

Vaughan Williams seldom theorizes; for him art is an important activity, something to be done, a work for hands and brain. "I have always found it difficult to study," he writes at p. 34 of this book. "I have learnt almost entirely what I have learnt by trying it on the dog." And later (p. 36): "I have learnt by trial and error; I have drawers full of these errors." Yet his work has never been empirical, never the work of a quack experimenting upon patients with new drugs. Rather he is like the craftsman whose first attempts were cast on the scrap-heap. One is reminded of Robert Louis Stevenson in *Memories and Portraits*: it could hardly be said of Vaughan Williams that he "played the sedulous ape," nor was he "known and pointed out for an idler"; but just as Stevenson in youth "lived with words," so Vaughan Williams has lived with music, and what he "thus wrote was for no ulterior use." Both sought always "the essential note and the right word: things that to a happier constitution had perhaps come by nature." "But this" (cries an arguer in Stevenson's essay) "is not the way to be original!" Stevenson adds that the student,

> before he can choose and preserve a fitting key of words, should long have practised the literary scales; and it is only after years of such gymnastic that he can sit down at last, legions of words swarming at his call, dozens of turns of phrase simultaneously bidding for his choice, and he himself knowing what he wants to do and (within the narrow limit of man's ability) able to do it.

The violin, not the pianoforte, we learn at p. 19, provided "musical salvation." Vaughan Williams is at base a melodic composer. Unlike Delius, his harmony comes out of his melody. The violin solo in *The Lark Ascending* has a singing quality; the melismas are vocal, apt though they be for the fingers stopping the strings. Folk-song naturally attracted this man of the earth because it was melodic. "The Joachim and Halir Quartets were at their zenith" in his youth, and he had by that time played tentatively in chamber music. On p. 24 he speaks of Parry's advice to "write choral music as befits an Englishman and a democrat." The great choral tradition of England is melodic, not harmonic, despite the Anglican chant; not only with "voice and verse" has Vaughan Williams sought his melodic ideal, but also in forging a singing part for an instrument, in bringing a voice into his *Pastoral Symphony*, in making his viola and 'cello and other inner instruments play parts far more vocal and expressive than the voice parts which Hindemith provided for his *Marienleben* songs. He may ask of his players something they are not accustomed to playing, but he asks nothing that, given the string range and pitch, choralists could not sing.

The reference to Raff's *Cavatina* is curious not as an example of Victorian taste, but in view of Vaughan Williams's later development. With slight exceptions, the music of the nineteenth-century composers seems to have passed him by, and, indeed, the music of most of the eighteenth-century composers too. His genealogical line springs from the Tudor school and English folk-song; there is an inter-marriage with Bach, but other composers are only among, not of, the family circle. It is hard to find a trace of admixture from Brahms, Schumann, or Beethoven. Even Schubert is only faintly felt; of the Liszt-Berlioz line rather less, except in the stage music. The aural suavity of that youthful but lovely-sounding trio *Sound Sleep*, for female voices, derives less from the tradition of Schumann and Brahms than from the words of Dante Gabriel Rossetti. But Vaughan Williams was not a Pre-Raphaelite for long!

The obvious exceptions may be noticed, the first of them Wagner. The young Vaughan Williams was endowed with a bubbling musical imagination; late in developing, he was unexpressive, almost incoherent, yet totally unwilling to write commonplaces, and determined to write what he found he meant. Such an ebullient soul would need to be encased in a body of tempered-steel plates if he were not to be swayed by the sheer sound, the endless flow, of Wagner's music as it poured over him. The fluency alone would be enough to cause, first, envy, and then liberation of speech. The influence had no lasting effects. When in a finished work (*A Sea Symphony*) some of that influence was manifested we find it in the oddest alliance with the American Walt Whitman. Even that universal-souled democrat, with the "thousand responses of my heart, never to cease, the million thence-aroused words," would not have expected to find himself remade, under the liberating influence of a German, into one of the sturdiest English works! As with Ravel, Vaughan Williams "*n'écrit pas la musique de*" Wagner.

More than one printed opinion has averred that *A Sea Symphony* shows the influence of Elgar. This I cannot observe at all. Vaughan Williams was untouched by the mid-nineteenth-century choral school, by the Three Choirs' Festival type of composition, by the anthem and the Anglican chant, least of all by the music of the Roman Church. He learnt, indeed, from the two Wesleys, especially the younger, who was a man of genius and stood apart. Vaughan Williams sought a lone path, one on which he often stumbled and lost his way, but leading him to his own, not to another's, truth. He learnt no set fine phrases, adopted no accepted system of musical manners.

Herzogenberg's remark (p. 30) about Mascagni was more penetrating than it may seem. It is doubtful if the young pupil had ever heard a work by Mascagni, but the comment foreshadowed what would, I suspect, have been thought of at that date by Vaughan Williams himself as an unlikely development, that of writing operas. Yet, many years later, several people, myself among them, have found here and there odd affinities of style between Vaughan Williams and Puccini, though no two composers could be more different in their ideals and beliefs in musical expression.

There is too much loose talk of the influence of one composer on another, as there is about 'cribbing' (p. 31). Too little attention is paid to the study of persistent idioms, trends of thought, that sweep across peoples and ages. The ordinary speech of our daily lives is gradually changing before our eyes, and the musical idioms of the day are bound to be reflected to some extent in the style of any but a consciously archaic writer. As Vaughan Williams himself once remarked, "Whenever a young composer writes worse than usual, the critics always say he was influenced by me!"

The greatest influence of all, probably, was Parry's "new idea"—"the loyalty of an artist to his art." Few in England in 1886 or so could accept, much less conceive, that thought. Parry wanted to write "music as his musical conscience demands"; but even for that vigorous pioneer the habits and usages of the day overweighted his busy life.

Leipzig was a musical Old Man of the Sea, clinging with sharp fingers to the necks of a multitude of Sinbads like a hundredfold hydra. The Leipzig ideals and insistence upon a central style in music, based on Haydn, Mozart, and Beethoven, had reduced many composers, not only English, to mere ciphers. Sterndale Bennett wilted in that admired conservatory to a pale Mendelssohnian sprig. Sullivan blossomed only in the Gilbertian *Singspiel*. Gade's talent was starved in the dominating town, and Grieg was only rescued from being a Kapellmeister-musician, a mere Nordic imitator—transformed into a true poet—by Richard Nordraak and Ole Bull. What those two did for Grieg, Vaughan Williams did mostly for himself. He was sufficiently tenacious and at the same time un-fluent to find his own idiom.

Music in England was taught in those days (and still is, to a large extent) in a foreign accent. Singers were directed to study for years all the sounds save those which occur in the English language. It was drilled into them that Italian first and German second were languages suitable for singing; English, the sung language of the madrigalists, of Campian, Dowland, and Purcell, was like the Doric lay of the uncouth swain in *Lycidas*. The staple musical diet was equally exotic: the studies of Nava and Clementi and Sauer led on to Haydn, Mozart, and Beethoven, Handel and Bellini, Schubert and Schumann, Wagner and Brahms and Verdi, with some Gounod added. Counterpoint was taught on the rickety rulings of Rockstro. The omissions make a startling list— Bach's Cantatas unheard, along with Wolf's songs; Berlioz and Liszt sharing a nebulous and forgotten country with Byrd, Monteverdi, Purcell, and the pre-Bachs. Above all other objects, education was directed towards the acquiring of a 'gentleman's accent,' which entailed the use of the language of the then accepted classics. Any other accent was regarded as impolite. The Covent Garden season won success only if the singers were aliens.

Into this curious welter of a German-thinking, Italian-

singing world came Vaughan Williams. The *Yellow Book*—
Beardsley and Wilde and Dowson—should here be recalled
to fill up a gap in the mental picture. Vaughan Williams was
a man who spoke the English language with a touch of
Gloucestershire accent. He had a firm mind, a creative
instinct, and no easy knack of tongue or pen. The world of
'English music' was not ready for *Façade* or *Peter Grimes*.
It was a challenging world, a world to conquer, for this
determined young man. Parry threw him a gage, and he
picked it up. During the later years he has shown himself
to be a champion of the English way. Joachim had to be
respectfully left behind; the English accent was of supreme
importance.

At once the point must be made that Vaughan Williams's
music is impolite. It conforms to no Leipzig standards.
His is no aristocratic muse: the goddess breathes her
inspired words through him without any Cambridge accent.
"Technique is the manners of music, without which it is
partly dumb," writes Fox Strangways of him.

> There are moments in his music, no doubt, when we are reminded
> of the walls of Tiryns, with blocks 10 ft. by 3 ft., bedded in clay;
> walls which, though the architect did not care much about technique,
> have lasted long enough for us to forget his name. . . . To be able
> to hold manners and character in equipoise is a gift of the gods.

To this study Fox Strangways sets an appropriate ending:

> hard, deep-seated Englishry, honest without gush, sensitive without
> lyrical rapture—there is in these [works] something that, like a
> course of Browning, corrects the Tennyson in us, and, learned or
> unlearned, invigorates us all.

One may be permitted to remember that G. K. Chesterton
characterized Tennyson thus: "He had a great deal to say;
but he had much more power of expression than was wanted
for anything he had to express. He could not think up to
the height of his own style."[1] Chesterton's other words on
Browning are supplementary. Of Browning he wrote: "His

[1] *The Victorian Age in Literature* (Home University Library, 1913).

eccentric style was more suitable to a nation of eccentrics. . . . Browning is the Englishman taking himself wilfully, following his nose like a bulldog, going by his own likes and dislikes." And if in Vaughan Williams's music we find occasionally Browningesque obscurities, where "the word with two meanings seems to mean rather less, if anything, than the word with one," we can continue with G. K. Chesterton's book in quoting his words that Browning "substituted the street with the green blind for the faded garden of Watteau, and the 'blue spirt of a lighted match' for the monotony of the evening star." No parallels between music and literature can be exact: indicative is the most hopeful adjective.

I am myself deeply convinced that the greatness of Vaughan Williams, his position in the gallery of England's great men, is not wholly dependent on the actual sounds he has invented for others to play and sing: sure that he is, extra-musically, a great man, linking our literature and our history and our singing into one great thing which is a part of our national life: certain that only by understanding the English ways of thinking and living shall any one of us understand the full greatness of our subject. The next chapter, therefore, is devoted to some exploration of the English people and their character in certain manifestations. We are reluctant, as a race, to analyse ourselves; but the inquiry into our Englishry is relevant to the study of this great figure who lives among us.

5

The English Background

UNDER the Norman conquerors (the dictionary tells us) the word "Englishry" meant "proof of English blood." That Vaughan Williams's music is "of English blood" none could doubt. But the process of analysis is elusive. No definition, no classification in a gallery of fingerprints, can pin down the Englishry of Vaughan Williams like a dead butterfly on the cork. He has given some hints, and it may be possible to gather a few more into a cloud of (unattested) witness. But while the scientist at his microscope may with patience and exactitude disentangle bacillus from bacillus, no investigator of the arts will reduce to formula or description in accurate words artists as different as Greco and Greuze, Flaubert and Forster, Dostoievsky and Dickens, Merimée and Meredith. As Sir Walter Raleigh pointed out in 1916,

> When a mathematician asks you to describe a circle, you create one. But the man who asks you to describe a monkey is less exacting: he will be content if you mention some of the features that seem to you to distinguish a monkey from other animals. Such a description must needs be based on personal impressions and ideas; some features must be chosen as being more significant than the rest.

Inquiry devoted only to the music, to the notes printed on the staves in the scores and sounded from time to time in our ears, will lead to no more than partial enlightenment. Rather, I suggest, we should pursue the longer road of English life and social history. The truth may shine clearly if we consider for a few moments six aspects of the English way of life: the English character and mind, the English

D   49

language, the English landscape, English folk-song, an earlier English music, and the English Church. These separate roads divagate in the prospect before us into cross-ways, tangents, high points whence other white ribbons of roads may be seen, some of them circling to rejoin the main highway.

Nationalism in music is a controversial subject. It is a characteristic of the English people that they are attracted by the national qualities of other nations but shy of their own. We readily accept the Dauphinois in Berlioz and the Basque in Ravel, the Spaniard in Falla and the Russian in Tchaikovsky. Far less readily do we appreciate the English-man in our own composers. Apart from the extended study of the general subject in his book *National Music*, Vaughan Williams treated it in a broadcast which he gave in December 1944.[1] Here are his own words for our guidance:

> That great historian of our own day George Macaulay Trevelyan once wrote that in the ideal world every nation would be different and all at peace; then he added (how prophetically!) that the modern tendency was for all nations to be alike and all at war. . . .
>
> It is quite true [the broadcast continues] that the greatest art transcends national frontiers, but it does not obliterate them. Shakespeare makes an international appeal for the very reason that he is so national and English in his outlook: Beethoven belongs to the whole world because he is first and foremost Teutonic. Certain foolish persons have called music "the universal language." There was never a more dangerous half-truth. Certainly the vocabulary of music is universal, but in terms of that vocabulary every community must make music which conforms with its temperament and traditions: otherwise it will be dead music. Is this parochial or narrow-minded? Well, let us be parochial and narrow-minded. It is the stream closely confined within its banks which acquires strength to turn the mill-wheel. When it overflows and spreads over the fields it forms a pestilential marsh.[2]

[1] It was the second of a series of four recorded talks on the North American Service: the titles were "The Musical General Practitioner," "Nationalism and Internationalism," "Rural Music," and "Making your own Music."

[2] See also "Who wants the English Composer?" (pp. 197–201 of the present book).

A very different view of nationalism in music is taken by Constant Lambert in his book *Music Ho!*[1] After calling Vaughan Williams's *Pastoral Symphony* "one of the landmarks in modern English music" he recalls that it received but little praise on its first performance, and adds that to a Czechoslovakian who dislikes it you can only say, "Oh, well, I suppose you don't like it." Lambert then goes on:

> Elgar's music is as national in its way as the music of Vaughan Williams, but, by using material that in type can be related back to the nineteenth-century German composers, Elgar avoids any suspicion of provincial dialect, even though his national flavour is strong enough to repel certain countries—France in particular.

No one would want to deny Vaughan Williams's English accent or his use of dialect. Nor do I for one contemn it. The point is, where are we to find the true nationalism? Am I to take it from Constant Lambert's words that the chorus "It comes from the misty ages," from *The Banner of St George*, is, because of its Victorian idiom, more centrally national than, say, the *Tallis Fantasia*? Are, in the truth of this age, the cuirassed figures of the Horseguard sentries in Whitehall, the changing of the Guard at Buckingham Palace, the Beefeaters with the Crown Jewels at the Tower, more national than "Gathering Peascods" or (for that matter) "Knees up, Mother Brown"? Is not this the attitude of the news reporter and the night sub-editor? And must it be applied, alone of all countries, to England? It all seems hopelessly out of date. The "English unofficial rose," which Rupert Brooke so longed for in the Café des Westens at Berlin in 1912, blooms for me in the *Serenade to Music* with a more natural scent than in any work of Elgar's.

Comparison with Kipling is not only inviting, but unavoidable, in this connexion. Modern criticism, as expressed by Bonamy Dobrée and T. S. Eliot, finds the essential Kipling in *Soldiers Three*. The Kipling of the vernacular personifies the common people in Mulvaney, Ortheris, and Learoyd; in them we are meant to find the

[1] Faber, 1934.

modern Everyman. Vaughan Williams is interested in every man and in his powers of musical expression. Elgar is more of an institutionalist, for whom the man in the street is an astronomical part of the Empire. Of the three, Vaughan Williams has the least of the orator about him; while Elgar set himself, with Kipling's "Fabulists," "to please," aware that "unless men please, they are not heard at all," Vaughan Williams struggled with his idiom to express a truth he had seen. Despite obvious external resemblances between Kipling and Elgar, my own opinion is that Kipling stands closer to Vaughan Williams. Comparing him with other poets contemporary with Browning, Dobrée says that Kipling "is more enduring, because something of the past three centuries clings to him." So it is with Vaughan Williams; his Englishry will survive because it comes from the English past.

The nationalism of Vaughan Williams grows from the earth. It comes from the people, though it may not be liked by the people; its roots are in what they wanted to sing then, though it may not be what they want to hear now. His nationalism is not negative; sometimes it is more positive than his æsthetic thought and his musical appeal to the public. It is never superimposed; not once in his career has he been an Englishman consciously. There is no *pastiche*, no strutting, no attitudinizing. Vaughan Williams does not deliberately mispronounce foreign words. Like the English, he is seldom intellectual; when his thought is remote he leads us rather into the distances of mysticism. His mind is no more smart than his clothes, and he dresses like a forgetful farmer. Not even in the stage works is there a trace of affectation. With all his stage sense, he brings to the theatre a breath of the open air. Maybe he speaks mainly from a world of horses and hay, of smells of living things, not from a world of metal cogs and plastics and mathematical precision-instruments, with the fumes of petrol hanging in our nostrils, nor yet from a world of incense. There are times when he drops into unrelieved dialect, as Kipling did into soldiers' slang. Like Chaucer's Friar, "Somwhat he lipsed . . , To make his English swete up-on his tonge." Let us so far allow Lambert his charge of "provincialism." But was there no provincialism in the Viennese idiom of Mozart and Beethoven? Many famous men have spoken English with a provincial accent; Hadow's Gloucestershire and Whittaker's Northumbrian were more native than Handel's or the Prince Consort's German-English. No one has cause to be ashamed of Hardy's peasants with their "nunny-watch" and "nammet-time," any more than they have of the "mingo" and "miching mallecho" of Shakespeare. Vaughan Williams's music may have a West Country burr, but at least it has not that distressing average of educated speech known derisively as the Oxford accent. His speech is direct and does not attempt to be persuasive, to convert us to his separate point of view. He speaks when he has a meaning, but, like Dr Johnson's Englishman, "is content to say nothing when he has nothing to say."

The sturdiness of the English tradition is the more curious on account of the mixture of races that goes to make up our blood. Celt and Saxon, Norman and Dane and Roman, German, even Phœnician, have contributed to our insular life and language. Out of this mingling of strains has come our peculiar doggedness, which at its worst becomes blind pertinacity. That doggedness, sometimes slipping down the slope into obstinacy, needs little demonstration in Vaughan Williams's music. With it goes a sense of loyalty unique among peoples, which can degenerate into an unthinking acceptance of tradition. The instincts of the British are towards liberality in all its senses, in social affairs, politics, and freedom of speech, for example; but their habits of thought, through their loyalty, are innately conservative. The Englishman is suspicious of sudden changes. He likes that which grows naturally, aided by skilful gardening and apt grafting: his roots are in the past, and he reveres the past with all his loyalty, longing for it to blossom naturally into the present, as he wants his own landscape to be natural in growth. Again, it is hardly necessary "to point the moral and adorn the tale" with quotations from Vaughan Williams's music. Any one work (quoted entire, of course) will show it, save perhaps the F minor Symphony, which is symbolic of the town rather than the countryside, and no less British for that, in these industrial islands.

Vaughan Williams's music can be called arboreal, essentially tree-like. Each work is a tree, a separate growth, different according to the circumstances of the soil, the predominant winds, proximity to river or sea, to mountain or moorland or town back-garden. His mind—his vision of beauty, if you like—drops a seed, which may be carried like a sycamore's on to soil different from that which nourished the parent. The seed does not always grow, but if it does it grows into something of the same genus but of individual shape as conditions prescribe. Each of his works has been allowed to grow to its own shape and size by the natural process of development, only influenced by the skilful forester's hand. His is no formal garden, but an open land-scape. I am reminded of the note by Evelyn de Morgan at the end of *The Old Madhouse*, the unfinished novel by her husband, William de Morgan. About his method of com-posing novels she writes:

> It was his practice to read out aloud to me every Sunday evening all he had written during the week. . . . As the story was always read to me while in progress I too got to believe in the reality of the characters, and found myself thinking of them as real people, and I have frequently asked him when he came down to lunch, or had finished writing for the day, such a question as, for instance, "Well, have they quarrelled yet?" and he would reply, as the case might be, "No, I don't know if they will come to a quarrel; after all, I must wait and see what they do."

The variations in Vaughan Williams's style and manner are due to his capacity for allowing his characters, or themes, to develop themselves, arboreally, into grown objects of recog-nizable shape, like a shrub or a human being. A Mongol is recognizably a man, of the same genus as an Englishman or a Kaffir. We do not, however much dictators may hope, grow up all alike. Nor have Vaughan Williams's works.

The Englishman has a love of truth and a healthy dislike of dogma. That is a part of our liberal-mindedness, and also of our independence. But with it go two other curiously opposite characteristics—a reliance on the instincts of a gentleman and an inability to see the truth in a flash. We pride ourselves upon being 'common-sense' people, and by common sense we really mean that sense, the English sense, which is extremely uncommon, and very difficult to define. Our public schools are based upon this tradition of fine instincts, and do not encourage hard thought about their purpose or results. Loving the truth, unwilling by nature to think what exactly the truth is, and untrained to discover it by an Euclidean, Ciceronic, or Voltairean logic, equally averse to Jesuitical and Calvinistic asseverations, we nevertheless somehow find the truth in the end.

Nothing less than the whole of Vaughan Williams's music is sufficient to exemplify this quality, which appears equally in his daily life. A more passionate lover of the truth never lived. He has unswerving determination to "follow the gleam." He has the tradition and the instinct to avoid will o' the wisps. He has the common sense to detect, and the simplicity of outlook to detest, shams. His career is in every way a Pilgrim's Progress towards truth, and he is as humble in his blunders as Christian, as likely to achieve both truth and beauty as that pilgrim by those very blunders, as uncertain and as persistent; and he has more capacity for humour. With dogged loyalty he continues the search. If he can find no other way, he makes a new expressive language, for he will hammer out the truth somehow, by persistence if not by flashing perception or ruthless logic. I have heard a famous musician complain impatiently of Vaughan Williams's "tortuous rectitude" in committee, and I have known cases myself where his obstinacy has been misunderstood by all who did not realize that the truth, however obscure, however much better left vague, was his only aim. Anyone who does not recognize the special truth of which Vaughan Williams has seen a glimpse, now in one guise, now in another, cannot hope to appreciate a single song, much less his noble series of symphonies. To think his philosophy or manner of expression mistaken is permissible, but to doubt his sincerity in the search is to be either perverse or blind.

The climate of the British Isles has always been a subject for humour in other countries. Yet the English are an out-of-doors race. "Mad dogs and Englishmen go out in the midday sun," wrote Noel Coward. The Romantic Revival was a back-to-Nature movement. James Thomson, and Haydn, watched the progress of the seasons from behind the protection of glass. But Thomas Gray stood in the Churchyard, and Housman was blown about on Wenlock Edge. William Blake heard the children's voices on the green and the laughter on the hill with his own ears, and Tennyson's line about "bowery hollows crowned by summer seas" gives an exact verbal picture of the effect, seen by the eye, of the sea over the rim of the lower-lying land, in the undulating country around Freshwater Bay.

The open-air-ness of the English peoples accounts for much in their tastes—for the Salvation Army, for example, for the fact that the local brass band of small provincial cities was, even in unregenerate days, far superior to the French *fanfare des pompiers*, for the popularity of the military band, and for the solemn organization of our processions—so unspontaneous and carefully regularized!

The point has æsthetic reference. The out-of-door life is healthy, sincere, muddy perhaps, but free from dust. It is like carpentry, firm and moderately exact: but it is not like illumination or silver-work—not perfect in detail and carefully cherished during the process of creation. We scan a five-barred gate from a distance, admiring its strength and the solidity of its morticing, and do not notice its rough edges, though we may hope we shall never, even in its decay, find a splinter in our fingers. To a glass showcase in a shop or a Hepplewhite cabinet in a drawing-room we adopt a different visual technique of judgement. We balance our eyes and mind instinctively.

Vaughan Williams is essentially an open-air composer. At his most mystical he is a pantheist among the Cathedral arches, a countryman walking in the nave. We must adjust our perspective, and expect from him something other than the exquisite marquetry of Mozart. The danger of this open-air-ness is, of course, clumsiness—of the heavy hand with the delicate screw, of the outdoor boots on the fine-pile carpet. That clumsiness Vaughan Williams does not manage always to avoid. It is to be accepted as an inevitable consequence of his mind and nationality; it is often a positive virtue.

The unadaptable, practical streak in the English outcrops at various surface points. 'Planning,' for example—we may talk of 'planning,' but we are in fact men of action first and consideration after. Of intellectual and artistic planning we are particularly suspicious, as the way we treat our artists shows. "Art for art's sake," said Vaughan Williams in *National Music*,

> has never flourished among the English-speaking nations. We are often called inartistic because our art is unconscious. Our drama and our poetry have evolved by accident while we thought we were doing something else, and so it will be with our music. The composer must not shut himself up and think about art: he must live with his fellows and make his art an expression of the whole life of the community. If we seek for art we shall not find it.

As he here spoke in words, so his music speaks.

A curious corollary, or manifestation, of the same trait is the popular delight in the elementary and the sentimental in music during hours of relaxation. Thus, the Victorian and Edwardian 'royalty' ballad was, from the eighteen-eighties to the nineteen-tens, the artistic equivalent of the evangelistic tract, with a touch of the girls' romantic penny tales about it. The stronger, the more iron-souled, was the business magnate, the more smoothly, it seems, was he engulfed in the mire of sentimentality of the home 'ballad.' He could criticize figures down to halfpennies by day; yet in the evening he could swallow lies about Bandoleros and Little Grey Homes in the West as if they were oysters in olive oil. Is not the crooner still with us?

From all kinds of sentimentalism Vaughan Williams mentally and physically recoiled: his palate refused it. His search for truth led him back to an earlier England, and those who complain of his 'medievalism' would do well to think of his strength of mind. His detestation of slush leads him sometimes to an austerity that is ineffective; yet *Linden Lea*, a song with genuine Dorset-dialect words by William Barnes and a tune that might be a folk-song but is not, attained 'ballad' status.

Our affection is deep, our love loyal and unstinted. In real affection we are unsentimental and silent; in love we are unexpressive (witness Trollope in his whole gamut from Mr Slope to Lord Silverbridge). We are nervous of speech in the presence of deep emotion, dumb, especially on the instant; now and then in a few words unsuited to epigram, in a few words of slang, we stumble upon a moving, even poetic, phrase. We are neither fluent nor glib. The House of Commons has been called the greatest debating society in the world, but the debates there are not always interesting to listen to. The spirit is magnificent, the semi-oratorical verbiage tedious. This Englishman's fear of words his oaths show, in their constant repetition to avoid more imaginative execration. 'Bloody' is a get-out, a way of escape from expressing a thought. A natural Nordic shyness may develop into an obstinacy of secretiveness, a pride in not giving anything away, in withholding vital points in evidence to a judge or in symptoms to a doctor. At the same time it seldom leads to introspection; for the Englishman is not normally a soul-searcher. The quality can, however, also turn swiftly into the opposite direction and beget the loud self-assertiveness of the inferiority complex.

Vaughan Williams has never been fluent in his use of musical language. He has an inexhaustible musical energy, a plentiful supply of ideas, but, even so, he has never found it easy to 'get it off his chest.' (The Holst "Field Days" must have helped him greatly.) About much of his music there hangs a certain mist of shyness, of tongue-tied inexpressiveness, only occasionally a lapse into 'take-it-or-leave-it' self-assertiveness. On his doggedness not the smallest work throws a shadow of doubt. The music comes to life for us, though there has perhaps been difficulty at its birth. As well try to rewrite it as to remould a difficult child by plastic surgery. What is, is, we seem to hear the music say, and, if it is not always quite up to Apollo's standard, it will be a good citizen, which is as much as most of us are and more than some. The music is human.

Common, and easy, criticism calls our natural distaste for eloquence one of the Englishman's 'limitations.' A true critical focus shows us not only the English limitations, but those of other countries and their composers—of Bellini and Strauss, Debussy and Bartók. Our lack of self-expression has virtues not known to all nations. A pleasant adjective for the attitude of mind is 'unassuming,' a word which implies not only a total rejection of the assumption of artificial or studied charm, but also a consideration for the tastes of one's interlocutor. If we English lack *chic* in dress and wit in conversation, in our literature we display a natural power of crystallizing quantities of wisdom within a short sentence. This power of distillation Vaughan Williams possesses to a surprising degree. It appears unexpectedly even in his immature works, where technique was tentative, and expression therefore too discursive for imaginative intellect to keep step. At its best this pregnant simplicity is startling, as in the second subject of the first movement of the D major Symphony.

Foreigners do not easily understand what are the English spirit of democracy and the English sense of freedom: they cannot accept, as logical deductions, the House of Lords on the one hand and our docileness under ridiculous petty regulations, form-filling, and by-laws on the other. Perhaps, through this unexplainable sense of historical democracy, Vaughan Williams shows his Englishry most firmly. He is, we know, at times a remote composer, in *Flos Campi*, in the *Magnificat* and the Piano Concerto. Yet it is true that his music is through and through saturated with the English people, with their native music, with their love of hymns, with all the fullness and all the limitations of their peculiar and complex character. Some one has said that national music is personal music tinged by the cultural background of a nation. If that be agreed it makes Vaughan Williams a true representative of the English peoples, for his culture is essentially that of his native country, while his music is as personal as if that country did not exist. He mingles the one individual consciousness with the conglomerate national consciousness.

More than any other composer since the Golden Age of the Tudors Vaughan Williams has been influenced by the English language. Milton's splendid sonnet on Lawes gives no just judgement. The bite of bow on string swayed Purcell more than the accentual incidence of his language. Parry, in his *English Lyrics*, could not shelter from the influence of Brahms. In Stanford's music only the vocal works show the linguistic direction of the new idiom. Yet in Vaughan Williams it is apparent in almost every phrase of his non-vocal works.

Let it not be thought that this affinity with the English language has been deliberately sought or cultivated by Vaughan Williams. Wide reader as he is, choosing poems for music from sources as distinct as John Skelton and Fredegond Shove, Dan Chaucer and Walt Whitman, he is not a literary man. Yet he has spoken to us in music of a kind that closely resembles our language, old rather than new. He feels the proximity of words to music, as the madrigalists did who wrote at the flowering time of English speech.

The English language, once mastered, is an enchanting medium of expression, but it can be as obstinate as a mule with those who think they know it merely from their education. Its disadvantages, as one would expect, are precisely those of the English people. Natural growth and graftings from French, Renaissance, German, and modern technical stocks have made it obscure to the English and nearly incomprehensible to other nationals. Under discipline, however, the English language is a living thing, as illogical as the English character, and as successful. In spelling alone it stands unique. Mr Shaw may convince us of the economic saving of improved orthography, but I hope and believe myself that the language will remain as it is. Artemus Ward spoke Anglo-Saxon sense when he said that "Chawcer was the wuss speler."

For all its contrariness, the English language is a beautiful, flexible medium, wayward (like our remaining lanes), happy in its dubieties, contradictory, a dangerous petard, used exquisitely by some and monstrously maltreated by other speakers and writers, an ancient treasure-house and yet a modern vehicle—a vehicle for thought whose wheels have been greased no doubt during the ages but still creak along and require no reflangeing of the Basic English kind to make it convey what is in Englishmen's minds to-day. There is a pleasure, one that never tires, in discovering how to use this loving, moving medium. It is a pleasure which the Civil Service has austerely put behind the filing cabinets, lest the jobs of the members might become personal and interesting.

Fowler's *King's English* and *Modern English Usage* check weeds that may stifle the continuing growth of our common means of communication. But neither those excellent books, nor Eric Partridge's, not even a study of the words in the *Oxford English Dictionary*—none of them will teach a writer to write fluid prose, to master his medium of words so that they flow from his mind as naturally as the ink from the rubber reservoir of his fountain pen. The practice of writing prose is the only means of learning to write prose.

Wondering, I have thought at times that the continual presence of the English language in his music has been the

greatest barrier against popular appreciation of Vaughan
Williams's work. We use our words so carelessly, care so
little for their beauty. Edward Thomas—then the new poet
"Edward Eastaway"—valued words and prayed for their
regard when he wrote:

> Out of us all
> That make rhymes,
> Will you choose
> Sometimes—
> As the winds use
> A crack in the wall
> Or a drain,
> Their joy or their pain
> To whistle through—
> Choose me,
> You English words?

Does not Vaughan Williams with equal humility seek
English sounds?

In any country town in England to sit quietly in a
pub and hear farm-workers talk is an education to a writer,
for they, in their simplicity and their traditional use of
our common language, utter phrases which no sophisticated poet could discover, thought he never so hard.[1] The
awkwardness of the provincial dialect, so disturbing to Mr
Constant Lambert, is the awkwardness of being able to
express oneself without training, or intellect, or education.
W. H. Davies had none but the peasant's or tramp's advantages, but he is among the poets of the English tradition.
He had in his soul the poetry that Shakespeare knew
Mistress Quickly would naturally speak when he gave her
the right words for Falstaff's epitaph. *Les politesses*, in set
phrases, can be learned by an actress, or a public schoolboy,
or a débutante, or a diplomatic clerk, or a jackdaw, in any
language, and can be made with a little skill to sound convincing in those places where such phrases please and do

---

[1] I heard one country woman in Worcestershire describe to her newly come
neighbour a farmer living near by. "He ain't a mucher," she said, which is a far
better and shorter phrase than to say, "He is of comparatively little account, and you
need take no notice of him." It also means more.

not irritate. The genuine spoken word comes from the heart.

Vaughan Williams's musical language is sufficiently akin to the English language to escape notice, like the Bible and our daily talk. We speak as we feel, unaware of tradition and too little informed by it. There is no literary language in England—we have no Mandarin tongue. The sailor may prize a parrot who swears in Swahili or Urdu, but he will not read a line of his native literature. In Vaughan Williams we hear the historic speech of the English peoples. What he gives us, in music, is the language of the breakfast table. It is also the language that Shakespeare wrote.

English is neither terse nor epigrammatic. It does not bubble, nor sparkle with laughter. Yet it is an admirable vehicle for puns, humorous verse, and nonsense rhymes. My aged uncle Arley, my aunt in Yucatan, the vicar who "slipped from politics to puns [and] passed from Mahomet to Moses," the dog that died, the heavy dragoon, the fol-de-rols and derry-derry-dandos and caleno custurume, are no less important a part of the heritage of literature than the sonnets of Shakespeare and Wordsworth, or than Shelley's *Prometheus*. Hilaire Belloc, born half French, and a French-speaker, adored our language that he adopted with such skill of absorption, and understood its genius for fun, even reviving the eighteenth-century type of epigram.[1]

More protracted than French, and less precise, our English language lacks the suppleness of ancient Greek, the rich rhythmic fluidity of Pindar. Italian is limpid, and has sweeter vowels and softer consonants, but wants our power of suggestion in short phrases; German is heavier but no less expressive. English moves slowly until it is wielded by a Gilbert—periphrastic by its very nature, awkward to manage, often vague and clumsy. On the other hand, what variety it can show! The richness of Spenser and Donne, the endless flow of Shakespeare, the elliptic obscurities of

[1] For example:
When I am dead, I hope it may be said,
"His sins were scarlet, but his books were read."

Meredith, vividness in Cobbett and Emily Brontë, raciness
in Smollett, the narrative style in Defoe and Dickens, the
classic dignity of Milton, the colourfulness of Tennyson, the
almost cubist angularity of Hardy's poems, the polished
jewels of Pater, the vulgar (but engaging) literalness of
Arnold Bennett, the punster-rhyming of Browning, the
crystal visual simplicity of Blake and W. H. Davies, the
subtleties of Jane Austen, the terrifying poise of Webster
and Marlowe, the comfortable jog-trot of Trollope, the
exquisiteness of Lytton Strachey, and, last to mention (for
one could fill pages with names), the unexcelled vigour and
comprehensiveness of the translators of the Bible. Especially
suited to verse in all shapes and rhythms, English is essentially
a language of speech and song, a point we forget. Our
poetry can be spoken aloud with an equal effectiveness to
that which it has in the silent-reading eye.

The music of Vaughan Williams contains many of the
advantages and awkwardnesses of the English language. His
"style is intimately connected with the inflexions and mood
of English folk-music." But folk-music has intimate connexion with the English language, for folk-music deals,
first, with words. His style, like our language, is intractable
but rich, uningratiating at first but sympathetic in the end.
We shall not find in one man all the variety of English as
she has been spoken through the ages—to expect in one man
the diversity of dozens would be absurd. On the other hand,
so fully have the varying lamps of our literature irradiated
his musical mind that in the very Englishness of his idiom
there occurs astonishing variety. His clichés are fairly
obvious; they come from our native speech. Haydn and
Mozart each had clichés. Our language is less polite and
ceremonial than theirs, no doubt, but I do not despise the
English or admire the eighteenth-century Viennese any the
more for that. I did not live in the Austrian Courts.

Alliteration apart, the passage from language to landscape
is no long a stair in the English house: so much in English art

is inspired and informed by the English scene. Only a fanatical ethnographer would seek to resolve national characters by climatic and geographical factors. Students of painting, on the other hand, are sensible of the effect of landscape on pictorial style, and literary critics give it heed in their judgements of poetry and prose. Far less attention is paid to the subject of landscape by writers on music. It was in derision, not sympathetic analysis, that Philip Heseltine described Vaughan Williams's *Pastoral Symphony* as "like a cow looking over a gate."

As I write these words I am sitting at a window in Worcestershire, looking out across the river towards Bredon Hill, plain to view, southward. I "watch the sunshot palaces high." The Avon here scarcely moves. So rich is the soil that the wild flowers and vegetables appear to have swifter upward motion than the lateral flow of the water. This, a voice says within, is no soil to breed Vikings or Goths. The progress of the years is slow; never sedate, but level in its unrolling. The unit of time is neither the minute nor the hour, hardly even the month: it is rather the season, as a climatic partition of the year. Antiquity might be ten years or a thousand behind us, as in Thomas Hardy's Dorset, so little do hills and valleys change. Here is a "country of easy livers, the quietest under the sun." Save for the recurring round of the year and the daily process of "getting and spending," "there is little that happens to one."

In a countryside not dissimilar, a few miles away, Vaughan Williams was born and brought up. His river was Thames, not Severn: "not London nor Knighton" his town. It is a landscape for thinkers and dreamers, a world fit for contemplation, a background against which personal display would be as unsuitable as a scarlet poster on a hoarding newly erected in a field, and youthful assertion of personal foible would look as ridiculous as a modern revue in the middle of an orchard.

When Vaughan Williams left this natural garden for a larger world he did not 'react' against it, as psychological

E

jargon would like us to expect. He took Gloucestershire with him, to Charterhouse and Cambridge, to the Royal College of Music and Berlin, much as Dvořák took Bohemia (and his family) with him to New York and Iowa. The West Country cannot leave his mind, because it is in his blood. There he saw the cow looking over the gate. I saw that same, that universal cow, only this morning. Vaughan Williams remembered it in London, and told us about it.

English landscape pervades his music, which tells us more of men and places, speech and song and the sky and the trees, than of fashions or wars, scientific developments, or revolutions, or the latest philosophies. Sometimes the hills are magnified by memory, the river runs swifter, the talk is wittier, than in the original. But seek for the crevasses of the Alps, the blue of Naples Bay, the fakirs or sand of the East, and you will not find them. One returning from the Southerly sun discovers that England is a little misty, low in colour values, but also exquisitely green, and moist, and rich in promise of harvest, with startling reds in the soil as against the ultramarine shadows on the yellow sandstone, and a beneficent, calm, persistent flora in compensation for the riotous purple creepers and the flaming bougainvillea. In art and music we each pick what we fancy, but we shall mistake the background of the creator's landscape if we demand from him colours his country cannot give.

Only a small part of Vaughan Williams's music could be called 'descriptive,' and not much more of it even 'illustrative.' The boxing match in *Hugh the Drover*, the chimes and the mouth-organ in the *London Symphony*, the clock in "The Water Mill," perhaps the melismatic cadenzas of the violin in *The Lark Ascending*, might qualify for the descriptive class. The *Pastoral Symphony* does not qualify even for the illustrative class, for we are given no clue save the vaguely comprehensive title to what the music is intended to illustrate; and the boisterous scherzo of the *Sea Symphony* is illustrative as much of the words as of the sea. The English coast and landscape are felt by us in their effects, but are not in any

sense portrayed by the composer. There is less picturesqueness in Vaughan Williams's works than there is in, say,
Falla's *Noches*. 'Impressionistic' is too marked an epithet
for anything but the earlier music, and ceases to have meaning at all as the style matures. Led though he may be by a
visual memory to set the mood of a movement or a piece,
within that movement or piece the composer is not diverted
by incidental moods from purely musical development. He
aims at, and achieves, absolute music, though it may perhaps
be conceded that he has an individual view of what the term
'absolute' means in music. Yet, all the time, the English
landscape forms the background to his dreams.

Of the influence of English folk-song, and to a less degree
English folk-dance, on this music little more need be said
here than has been said by the composer himself (p. 32 *ff.*);
that little is corollary upon the paragraphs about the English
language. It has long been fashionable to overrate the folk-
music influence—indeed, to write as if every bar by Vaughan
Williams is reminiscent of folk-song, and as if he had used
our corpus of traditional music as a reserve supply of thematic
ideas when his own spring of melodic invention had run
dry. In fact, Vaughan Williams's direct quotations from
folk-music, except in avowed *quodlibets* and arrangements,
are oddly scanty. Moreover, this overstated influence is
not seldom referred to in a derogatory spirit.

It has always eluded me why Balakirev and Borodin,
Kodály and Bartók, Falla and Grieg, should be permitted by
English judgement to display their folk-song badge openly
on their breasts to the admiration of the public, while
Vaughan Williams in doing so requires some kind of
apology. Vaughan Williams is influenced by English folk-
song just as Bach was influenced by the Lutheran chorale,
and Sir George Dyson has pointed out "an English Bach
would have used these idioms as his predecessors the Tudors
had done."[1] "Intimately connected with the inflexions and

---

[1] *Cecil Sharp*, by A. H. Fox Strangways and Maud Karpeles, Appendix, p. 215.

moods of English folk-music"—the phrase quoted before from Constant Lambert hits it off exactly. Vaughan Williams makes free use of the traditional vernacular of the English people, which includes (*pace* Stanford) the flattened seventh, among other elements sometimes overlooked, like vocal freedom of rhythm. Nor should it be assumed that English folk-song is limited to one mood or manner; it is, in fact, a complex anthology of widely varying moods and idioms. The fingerprint folk-song pressed upon Vaughan Williams's mind is most easily to be recognized in his liking for the full tone, not only in cadences, but also in melisma and arabesque, in cast of melody and movement of harmony. The trend of general musical thought has for long generations slid away from the full tone; we find to-day that the semitone, with its reverse, the major seventh, is as unmistakable a fingerprint of William Walton as the full tone is of Moeran and Vaughan Williams.

The six categories into which at pp. 49-50 the English background was arbitrarily divided for purposes of discussion do not separate themselves like so many pieces of type in a composing stick or a row of loaves of bread in a baker's window. The vignette edges begin, as we come to the last two—old music and the English Church—to blur and merge with those of their surrounding neighbours. It is equally difficult and unnecessary to try to decide where a well-designed pattern on a textile or a wallpaper begins and ends, so long as it covers the surface meaningly.

The gap between folk-music and what is called, comprehensively and vaguely, 'old' music is palpably smaller than that between folk-music and 'classical' music. Our earlier cultivated or (detestable phrase) 'art' music is cousin germane to the music of the people, different circumstances naturally shaping the practice and development of each in its own way. No reference to 'old' music is made by the composer save where, at p. 24, he attributes to Parry his own inheritance of the legacy of "the great English choral tradition" from

Tallis to the Wesleys, and onward. No doubt Parry sowed the seed: the germination and flowering were a process entirely individual to Vaughan Williams. The English choral school of the sixteenth century afforded him a model for freedom of rhythm, suppleness of phrasing, unsquareness of balance in phrases. It liberated him from the youthful composer's common (and catching) disease of four-bar-itis. The oddly swift decline of the polyphonic style of composition gave easy passage of entry into music of the rhythms of the dance—body rhythm rapidly supplanted speech rhythm. Vaughan Williams has always reacted against the potency of body rhythm (even in *Job*), and it seems certain that we have to thank the 'old' music more than folk-song for this. Another important portion of the legacy was a growing interest and a developing skill in writing a rich and moving contrapuntal texture, the latter not being fully attained until comparatively late in life, with such works as *Five Variants of "Dives and Lazarus"* and *Household Music*. The word 'rich' does not imply harmonic richness: indeed, from the same inheritance Vaughan Williams learned a curious bareness and sometimes even austerity of harmonic style. His music tends to be woven rather than sewn, to quote his own description in *Grove* of the fugue as against the sonata, and this weaving is one source of the wealth of his rhythmic patterns.

The earliest full manifestation of the older influence appears in the *Fantasia on a Theme of Thomas Tallis*, one of Vaughan Williams's important early works, first heard under Sir Thomas Beecham in Queen's Hall, London, in 1910. Thirteen years later he showed how he could re-create the polyphonic English style as a subtle medium for his own thoughts, in the Mass in G minor, which he wrote, at the repeated demand of Sir Richard Terry, for the choir of Westminster Cathedral. Later still, in the opera *Sir John in Love*, he performed another feat of re-creation. While Boïto and Verdi made out of Shakespeare's Falstaff an eternal work of art, a superlative opera, Vaughan Williams has quite simply translated Shakespeare into music—not, be it noted, into Italian or into the language of operatic convention. The words as well as the spirit of the age of Shakespeare are fully presented to us in music. Not one bar is *pastiche*; there is none of that raffishness which gives *Pétrushka*, as played in the concert hall, the jaded, artificial appearance of the made-up film actor lunching in the studio restaurant. In this opera the two earlier musics of England meet, the music of the aristocrat and the music of the peasant: they meet in the soul and the score of a living Englishman, who has an innate understanding of Shakespeare, his librettist, and yet lives among us now.

For the sixth and last source of Englishry in Vaughan Williams's music I named 'the English Church.' His list of works might suggest that 'the Christian religion' would be a more appropriate phrase. Illogically, I find the first phrase the more comprehensive description, the part for once comprising and defining the whole. Of conventional Church music Vaughan Williams has written little. The hymns and carols are important in a way (one hymn especially so); there are some anthems, the larger *O Vos Omnes*, some festival works, and the really big Mass in G minor: the field is covered. We know from his own words how unsuited he found himself to the organ loft. The Anglican Church tradition of the nineteenth century provides but one more example of how a hundred-and-more years of music, with its vagrant moods and fashions, flowed by him without marking the banks of his Western stream. When he has turned to Holy Writ he has used the words for non-liturgical purposes—in *Sancta Civitas*, for example, or the *Benedicite* and *Magnificat*. The English choral tradition flew, as on wings, from past ages, alighted for a while's rest on the Wesleys, and sang its song to him through Parry's mouthpiece. Vaughan Williams has been much performed at the Three Choirs' Festivals; but he is as remote from Sir George Martin and Sir John Stainer as he is from Clementi and Spohr.

The tradition of the English Church, as a part of English

life, speaks in Vaughan Williams's music in unconventional phraseology. For a purely personal impression, I find myself continuously and unconsciously associating in my mind the composite visual image of our Church architecture with the composite aural memory of this music. I can feel at times the village Church of the earlier centuries, standing always near water and with the farm or manor next door—the symbol of the English village: at times I could imagine myself in Abbey or Cathedral, with the loving variety of carved boss and capital, the Decorated vaulting poised on earlier Norman arches, clerestory and lantern and flying buttress around me. No direct comparison is to be built on a personal feeling. Yet it cannot be denied that the Nordic arch and column give firmer basis to this musical architecture than the ogee, the mosaic, or the gilded splendours of the baroque or Byzantine styles. Such of the stream of plainsong as has trickled through into his music (in *Riders to the Sea*, for example) comes from the simpler spring of Sarum (or English) usage. One is conscious of profound religious convictions; one is equally conscious of an absence of ritualism.

Vaughan Williams's important contribution to the music of the English Church lies in the area of hymnology. Editor of the music in *The English Hymnal* (1907), part-editor of *Songs of Praise* (1925) and *The Oxford Book of Carols* (1928), he has exercised with his editorial skill, and with a handful of hymns of his own composing, a far greater and more salutary influence on English Church music than any composer since Wesley. He himself has recognized (p. 34) the value to his musical education of that year or two of studying hymns. We may be allowed, perhaps, to expand his words a little. Of all choral music the hymn is the most democratic. It is the central expression of the people's part in worship. As long ago as 1906 Vaughan Williams wrote the noble tune *Sine Nomine* as a communal setting of the words "For all the Saints who from their labours rest." Two distinct strands can be discerned in these hymnological labours—the influence of Bach and the influence of folk-music. Bach's idiom, we know, came to him as something instantly recognizable. The dignity and firmness of the Lutheran tradition of the chorale, and Bach's use of it, could not but interest and inspire this particular mind. On the other side, the natural gaiety, spontaneity, and modernity of feeling in the carol could attract him no less. Priest and layman come together in this religious but not sacred music.

No assault will be attempted here on the process of English thought and expression in religion. The defences of the subject are impenetrable; the outlying ramparts and traps waiting for the assailant are complicated and well hidden—plainsong and the decorous rhymed psalter of the Puritans, *Everyman* and Dorothy Sayers, Purcell's "Bell" Anthem and Bax's *Mater, ora filium*, black gown and bands alongside Eric Gill's sculptures, and Walmisley's anthems alongside Charles Williams's *Cranmer of Canterbury*. No clear path can be easily picked through the maze. Confronted, however, with the sight of a religious Englishman expressing himself in an act of devotion but not of ritual, I am tempted to refer the reader to Sir Herbert Grierson. His introduction to the anthology which he entitled *Metaphysical Poetry of the Seventeenth Century—Donne to Butler* provides a short analysis of this side of the English expressive mind. The verse itself is exquisitely beautiful for those who can accept its fantasies, its obscurities, its avoidance of direct statements, as part of the English dislike of publicly expressed religious fervour (save in the singing of hymns). These poets, writes Grierson, in all their vagaries, "succeed in stumbling upon some conceit which reveals a fresh intuition into the heart, or states an old plea with new and prevailing force." We find (in his words) "passionate, paradoxical argument, touched with humour and learned imagery." Underneath all this Grierson observes and emphasizes "the note of conflict, of personal experience, which troubles and gives life to poetry that might otherwise be too entirely doctrinal or didactic."

None of the post-Mendelssohn, comfortable, successful, Victorian Anglicism could satisfy Vaughan Williams: his mind moved less complacently, back to an earlier Church of England, to a less glib means of expression, to a deeper thought and a profounder art, a more native method (albeit more shy) and a cleaner idiom of expression. Within Vaughan Williams's music the 'metaphysical poets' are contained. Theirs was, to be sure, an age of 'conceits,' of poetic flowers springing untended from every shoot on their stems; and the ages (multiple and quickly changing) in which Vaughan Williams has lived are marked out by their paucity of faith, their bareness of human supplies, without which a glory of imaginative invention[1] is not to be expected. Of direct similarity in style between those poets and Vaughan Williams there is no more than there is between him and the Tudor madrigalists. Yet the family likeness is obvious. One poem of George Herbert's will, perhaps, elucidate my point.

Easter Wings

Lord, who createdst man in wealth and store,
Though foolishly he lost the same,
Decaying more and more,
Till he became
Most poore:
With thee
O let me rise
As larks, harmoniously,
And sing this day thy victories:
Then shall the fall further the flight in me.

My tender age in sorrow did beginne:
And still with sicknesses and shame
Thou didst so punish sinne,
That I became
Most thinne,
With thee
Let me combine,
And feel this day thy victorie:
For, if I imp my wing on thine,
Affliction shall advance the flight in me.

[1] The recent desire for the mere verbal richness of John Donne is paralleled in music by the successful new career of the Romantics (particularly Tchaikovsky) in England to-day. It has no religious or mystical basis whatsoever, as far as I can judge.

The figuration in the shape of the hour-glass has many parallels in music, from Okeghem to Schumann: the fugue is a pattern before it can be expressive.

Though, in fact, little of such technical rebus-making occurs in Vaughan Williams's works, there are many traces in them of a desire for older forms than those of the expressive outpourings of Romantics. But "most poore" is what strikes my eye and ear—this crystallization of thought upon one phrase. It is continually apparent in him. He wishes to "rise as larks, harmoniously": actually he naturally rises melodically, but desires the harmony too: he could "sing this day thy victories." He is opposed, equally with Herbert, to the "affliction" and its "flight in me"—he longs for no introspection or inquiry into his soul. This music and this verse share the same combination of humour and seriousness, of earnestness of purpose and gentleness of touch, of intense meaning underneath lightly treated words. The parallel is not precise, but sufficient if we remember the differences of the centuries.

This mystical outpouring of Vaughan Williams's I would count as one of the important parts of his Englishry— perhaps the summary of all the other parts of that Englishry —character, language, landscape, folk-song, and old music. In this outpouring some of his finest imaginative works flow over us. Even when he is least mystical the spray from the stream still flecks him. We are at the hub of Vaughan Williams's wheel (though I remind you of the felloe, the flange, and the spokes) when we couple his name with that of George Herbert.

Music speaks to us in its own language. Words can do no more than try to describe the background before which the music stands, erect and firm, in its own nobility of person. To those who, at the end of a literary passage, seek closer relationship between my words and Vaughan Williams's music, I would "point the moral and adorn the tale" by directing their eyes and ears to the last of the *Four Hymns*, for tenor voice, viola, and strings. The words of the fourth are by Robert Bridges, of the other three by Bishop Jeremy Taylor, Isaac Watts, and Richard Crashaw respectively. Conceived before the First World War, the cycle was performed in 1920 at the Worcester meeting of the Three Choirs' Festival, and was published the same year. It is dedicated to "J.S.W."; he may be taken to be the tenor singer who, as Sir Steuart Wilson, has been directing the music at the British Broadcasting Corporation.

This neglected setting of Bridges's adaptation of an old Greek hymn is an artistic achievement of major importance. It is beautiful; and it is also typical. It sums up the Englishry of the man who composed it, with all the awkwardness and charm, the narrowness and the spaciousness, the obstinacy and the flow, the shyness and the love, which are, I hope, parts of our patchy national character. The pen itches to analyse it bar by bar. Common sense recommends that the song be left to display its own breadth, its own musical joy in words like "splendour," "adoring," "holy," and "exalt," its own glow of colour, not to be mixed in others' studio or laboratory.

Out-of-door carpentry, perhaps, it is. For myself, I feel I am standing outside a massive building, enjoying the smooth, living grass in the precincts and hearing this elemental song come to me through the stained glass of the windows as I stand in the sun and air. I am filled with naturalistic adoration. An ancient voice is "crying and calling to me," the voice of a man alive in my day who can speak, in intelligible language, of England's history, of her men and women and her slowly changing landscape. Other and older voices sing in worship as this song rolls out its simple pattern.

So frequently has reference been made in these foregoing pages to the past that it is, perhaps, necessary to anticipate the question, "Is this music by Vaughan Williams in tune with the times in which we live?" Even such meagre belief in progress as I hold leads me to the view that his lifelong utterance has that especial mixture of the personal and the universal from which prophets and seers are compounded— Bunyan and Elijah, Homer and Ezekiel. That it is not listened to in our time as much as it should be is an apparent fact. But then the English people are notoriously shy of the English manner of thought and life, suspicious (shall I say?) of themselves and their fellow-men. Recognition of an alien accent, of Tchaikovsky's and Fauré's, to quote two recent examples of public acceptance, comes slowly perhaps, but comes more easily than the recognition of vernacular greatness. "There are nine and sixty ways of constructing tribal lays, And every single one of them is right."

6

A Brief General Survey of the Works

THE list of the writings of Ralph Vaughan Williams printed, for the first time, at p. 204 *et seq.* of this book is long, but not so depressingly long as that of many other and lesser composers; indeed, it is more lively and interesting on the surface than many musical bibliographies, which as a rule make dull reading; for there is an engaging variety of titles, poets, subjects, sizes, and mediums. Many of the listed works are discussed in these pages; for a moment or two it may be permitted to consider the list as a whole.

The relative dimensions of the works, for example, are worth study. The gamut extends from full-length operas down to school songs, carols, and hymn-tunes. A corollary of this dimensional variety is the large number of musical forms that the composer has adopted. There is almost everything one can think of, except the solo sonata, which does not occur so far. Among standard musical forms we find symphony, concerto (in different kinds), string quartet and quintet, suite, fugue, *passacaglia*, Mass, motet, chorale prelude, song and song-cycle, next to chamber opera, grand opera, comic opera, ballet, and film-music. The more conventional types of composition are not in the majority, and are mostly used with individuality. Of form in the sense of treatment, as a medium in the painter's sense, there is an exceptional range.

The voice, it is not surprising, comes in for the most varied handling. Apart from the usual songs, and the solo parts in the operas and the choral works, we find both solo and choral singing used in fresh and interesting ways. For example, there is a set of songs for voice and violin alone,

77

as well as the unaccompanied soprano solo opening and closing the last movement of the *Pastoral Symphony*. A good deal of this music is designed for wordless and even background chorus. In the early *Willow Wood* a choir of sopranos and altos provides a setting for the baritone solo. *Flos Campi* is entirely wordless. The *Magnificat* is for flute solo and female-voice choir. The "*Six Choral Songs*, to be sung in time of war," are intended for massed unison singing, while the *Three Children's Songs* were written for young voices. The *Serenade to Music* is for sixteen solo voices and orchestra. *Sancta Civitas* and *Dona Nobis Pacem* require large choral forces, just as the Mass in G minor is unsuited to anything but a small picked choir. And this rich store of vocal colouring is added to by the folk-song arrangements for solo or for various choral bodies or for both.

Instruments fare less well, but even so there is a generous provision. The full orchestra is vanguard to a procession of works for double string orchestra, string orchestra and harp, and military band: concertos for violin, for pianoforte, and for oboe: and miscellaneous works for violin, etc. The viola has had special attention, with *Flos Campi*, the Suite for viola and orchestra, and the string quartet with viola lead. Chamber music is sparse, but includes the short song-cycle *Merciles Beauty*, scored for string trio, and *Household Music*, which can be played by almost any conceivable combination of instruments that happen to be gathered together in music-school, army hut, or club-room. There is a marked shortage of works for keyboard; a mere handful of pieces for organ and for piano, none of great account—the only outstanding keyboard work is the Piano Concerto. Of formal Church music there is little: yet a strong mystical or religious vein runs through the whole of the music. For the stage there are (to date) three grand operas, two chamber operas, an *opera buffa*, incidental music, a large ballet, and two folk-dance ballets; for the photographic stage several film scores. In his provision for the dance Vaughan Williams obviously drew more upon the English folk-tradition than upon the

French and Russian traditions of the theatre. Into the cinema set he walked with no more preconceived ideas than those of his ordinary idiom and experience, and began to learn his technique anew at the age of seventy.

Few works owe their origin to commissions; indeed, only two important works, the *Serenade to Music*, designed for Sir Henry Wood's Jubilee with his exacting demands as to voices to be used, and *Thanksgiving for Victory*, written for broadcasting; on the other hand, quite a number of pieces have been written for specific purposes—for the Leith Hill Festival, perhaps, or at the repeated request of a soloist, or for an assembly or congregation in Church to sing, or for a film.

The choice of words to be sung is interesting; Whitman, Housman, and the metaphysicals (especially Herbert) seem to take place even before Shakespeare. The Bible is a frequent source. Stevenson and Shelley and Skelton jostle the modern Seumas O'Sullivan. Dante Gabriel Rossetti had his own period of favour. Nowhere do we find poor or silly words accepted by this composer. Even in the lighter-weight works the literary taste is of high standard, and the same thing can be noticed in his titles, which are simple, direct, and sincere.

The dates are illuminating. At first the orchestral works are tentative, the vocal works successful, especially the choral works. As the orchestra has risen in popularity in England, so has Vaughan Williams shown an increasing interest in the wholly orchestral medium. A return to choral writing can be seen at times, but not in the persistence of the earlier period. There seems to be no cycle of recurrence in the mystical mood's appearance. It is continually in the background.

Actuarial analysis would no doubt reveal many other points of interest in the factual catalogue. What it could not disclose, as the scores themselves do, is the growing rise in technical fluency until, in the later works, it becomes a great craftsman's unconscious mastery of the musical mediums. The progress was not the result of a strategical campaign, of a planned policy. It was a natural growth from seed to tree, and of such things bibliography cannot take account.

7

The Earlier Works

O F the earlier works—that is, those that came before the first completed version of *A London Symphony* in 1914—some have been destroyed, some revised. Those that are withdrawn are not discussed here[1]; to drag up skeletons of the past would be at best a task for a prying biographer, at worst a task for a musical resurrection-man. The whole period is one of discovery: the composer was pursuing an uncharted path, and we are following the trail left by his footsteps. Not every by-way will take us to an equally interesting end, but we can avoid cul-de-sacs with care. It should not be forgotten that a number of these pre-1914 pieces attained a popularity seldom accorded to the later works—many, indeed, keeping their public hold to the detriment of their successors.

Before the Walt Whitman stage is reached two poets seem especially to have appealed to Vaughan Williams's musical imagination—Dante Gabriel Rossetti and Robert Louis Stevenson. From the former he took one set of verses for a female-voice part-song, and no less than ten sonnets, six of them made into a song-cycle called *The House of Life*, and the other four into a work for chorus and orchestra, *Willow Wood*. Out of Stevenson's verses he made the two books of *Songs of Travel* (1905 and 1907 respectively) and one separate song, *Whither must I wander?*

Sound Sleep, from the early Rossetti period, is an innocent, youthful trio, which sounds quite lovely on voices and is oddly conventional in its romanticism.

---

[1] Stanford wrote in a letter of 1899: "I heard yesterday a *Serenade* by Vaughan Williams, a most poetical and remarkable piece of work."

The House of Life is of far greater interest, not only because it contains one of the few songs by Vaughan Williams known to every singer and singing-teacher, and attempted by every singing-pupil, much to its disadvantage: "Silent Noon." One of those unpredictable whims of public taste elected that this song should so stand out from the cycle that one has literally never known two singers perform any of the others, and met but few who had bothered to look at them. The cycle as a whole has considerable merit. It is discussed here in some detail as a seeding nursery for many later flowerings, and therefore important for those who would study Vaughan Williams's mind.

The sonnet's "scanty plot of ground" has always been hard for the composer to fertilize musically: "with this key Shakespeare unlocked his heart," no doubt, but it has not had the same "Open Sesame" effect upon composers. The form, self-contained as the fugue, appears to be too large for a song, and yet as "a moment's monument" too small for extended treatment. The scheme of eight plus six lines has no counterpart in music.

Rossetti did not simplify the verbal pattern of the sonnet's shape. To Shakespeare's fluent imagery, Milton's "soul-animating strains—alas, too few!" and Wordsworth's delight in his "convent's narrow room," Rossetti added a new, post-Goethe, post-Shelley, nineteenth-century florid imagery of his own. It has been shrewdly said (I would gladly acknowledge if I could remember by whom) that Rossetti was literary in his paintings and pictorial in his poems. We find in this sonnet-sequence an astonishing mixture of solid substance ("the golden kingcup-fields with silver edge, where the cow-parsley skirts the hawthorn hedge") and visionary, visual figures like the "flame-winged" who, "brought a white-winged harp-player." We veer from the corporeal "gold bar of Heaven" on which the Blessed Damozel "leaned," to the "image of Life's retinue that had Love's wings and bore his gonfalon." Unlike Midas, we touch the object, and the gold becomes "the ground-whirl

F

of the perished leaves of Hope." Reality and unreality interweave in Rossetti's sonnets, like the shavings in Holman Hunt's painting of the Young Christ in the carpenter's shop. The splendour still glows for me; does it, too, for others younger than I?

The complicated problem of setting to music a mere six sonnets selected from a sequence of a hundred and two—each one in the sequence itself a complex work of art half dependent for its emotional pattern on its neighbours—Vaughan Williams attacked with an adventurous Quixotry more common in men of twenty than of thirty years of age. His musical assault was planned on a large scale. It was (and still is) customary in England to believe that large musical conceptions demand large forces for their realization, despite the plain evidence to the contrary given by Schubert, Wolf, and Warlock. Vaughan Williams's campaign on Rossetti is original and, I feel, successful. There were certainly no songs being written at the moment of creation which bore any resemblance to these six of *The House of Life*. For all its confinement to two performers, the work is plainly a musical achievement of greater dimensions than the choral-orchestral *Willow Wood*.

The leit-motive at the opening recurs in *Willow Wood*. There is a lovely *andante* poise about the first part of the song, the piano playing an important rôle. Then follows an interesting phrase. In that early "moment of vision" the common chord is reconceived. Vaughan Williams's new common chord is not always, or even usually, in "root position." The form of the song is rounded off with a development and recapitulation of the vocal tune scored for piano; at the end of the words the voice ceases and the music runs on naturally in the piano—an interesting method of squaring the two circles of sonnet and song, but not one which all singers could support with dignity on the platform. Of "Silent Noon" it is safe and politic to say that it is the best song of the six, certainly that one which shows the firmest manner of presentation. It is well registered and well constructed; and if it does not clasp me to its heart, at least the dragonfly hangs like a blue thread. The winged hour dropped from above is, I find, a little too much for the average English singer's range of expression.

"Love's Minstrel" is at once the weakest song in the cycle and a fine declamatory singer's song. Here we can find the first traces of Vaughan Williams's narrative style, so successfully developed later in the stage works and the Symphonies. The poem introduces a solid but mysterious harp-player, who at the beginning of the third line is presented to us in person, in the one word "saying." We drop into *oratio obliqua*, which, by the time the singer who knows no Rossetti (save possibly *Beata Beatrix*) presents it to an unlettered audience, becomes remote. The far-away-ness is not lessened by the composer's rather wintry use of plainsong idiom. The false relations of sharp and natural presage better usage of the chromatic idiom in later works. And is Rossetti's Love with his wan water and wan moon the same Love who bids us welcome in the *Five Mystical Songs*? I judge not.

The fourth song wears the garb of popularity, but never has attained the status of its robes. As a youthful indiscretion (so, I believe, the composer regards it) it is as good as the earlier Sibelius and Elgar works; even so, I find it fresh and engaging—a delightful platitude. The dramatic section of the composer's mind was brought into operation here, but there was no dramatic outlet for Englishmen in Vaughan Williams's youth. *Aut Wagner, aut nihil*; and Wagner was not a nice Englishman who produced Greek plays on the lawns at Cambridge, but a professional German whose operas we proudly bought. There is beauty here, neverthe-less, and I decline to define beauty.

"Death in Love," the next song, clearly announces itself as a sketch for a larger canvas. The spaciousness is that of Rossetti, not Whitman. The pianoforte is the wrong medium here, for tonally it can only shadow in the splendour necessary for "the image in Life's retinue" (whatever he may have looked like with his "gonfalon" and "semi-sequestered face"). Three trumpets would seem to offer a more suitable megilp, but the fanfare had not at that period become a fashionable form for young composers. The vocal style is declamatory, exact to the demands of the poem, and there is a harmonic presage of the B flat–D major progression which opens the *Sea Symphony*.

Tinged with Wagnerean colours as it is, the last song of the cycle ("Love's Last Gift") is by no means the least typical or the least English, and is the largest in scale of the six. It leads us by an easy path from the highly coloured, literal Rossetti to the airier, vaguer Whitman. The broad simplicity of the main tune foreshadows Fenton's great song in *Sir John in Love*. Previously stated ideas are recalled for new development, and the ending has the rare nobility of Vaughan Williams's later music. As in other early pieces by the composer, the middle section is the weakest, suffering to all appearance from cramp.

The House of Life, despite youthful indiscretions, contains so much evidence of the composer's early aspirations, of that splendid creative enthusiasm which has lived on in the man far into his ripe years of maturity, that I commend it to seekers after his truth, in the hope that they will find in it, as I do, a glow brighter than that in some of the more readily accepted later works. The English landscape is coming up before us, even in this beginning.

Willow Wood, a "cantata for baritone solo with accompaniment of orchestra and chorus of sopranos and altos (*ad.. lib.*)," puts into music as a collected whole four more sonnets by Dante Gabriel Rossetti. "And still Love sang, and what he sang was this." The third sonnet gives his song, which the ladies' chorus sings, hitherto having had no more to articulate than "ah" and the two words, "for once." The soloist has a counter-melody, and it seems doubtful if the words of Love's song will be audible until, at the sestet, the soloist sings them alone. The work as a whole is a good deal less successful than *The House of Life*, from which it borrows a phrase as its opening orchestral figure, later developing it with some elaboration, bowed by the weight of its stiff clothes. The theme of Love's song is the second main idea, and here we find Vaughan Williams wrenching the words and their proper accentuation to his musical purpose, a practice uncommon in him. As the completion of the Rossetti phase, and as an example of Vaughan Williams's earlier methods of musical development, *Willow Wood* has interest, and much of the choral writing is effective.

Of the two books of *Songs of Travel*, to Stevenson's words (taken from the little volume of the same name), the first, containing "The Vagabond," "Bright is the Ring of Words," and "The Roadside Fire" (the composer's not the author's title), won for itself and still keeps a considerable popularity. The second book attracted far less attention, and is not remembered now. The popularity is easily understood, though it is the outcome of a number of contributory causes. The songs were dedicated to and sung by Harry Plunket Greene, who, with Gervase Elwes, was in the forefront of the battle for the revival of English song. In the 'eighties and 'nineties, when Parry and Stanford were inaugurating the movement with their own clean, vigorous, and sensitive treatment of English poetry, English song had sunk into the deepest abysses of insincerity and ineptitude. Harry Plunket Greene was an important exponent of the proper union of poetry and music[1]: he made sense of the songs he sang, and with high imaginative powers was scornful of the high-falutin' rubbish then in fashion.

Stevenson's verses had a wider vogue then than they have to-day, though there are signs of a revival of interest. His words Vaughan Williams treated audibly and with literal regard for their meaning, inflecting his music to the poet's demands. The music is picturesque, in the sense of illustrating the poems' meaning. He produced the exact equiva-

[1] Compare *Singing learnt through Speech*, by Edward C. Bairstow and H. Plunket Greene (Macmillan, 1946).

lent in music of the quick sketch, the thrown-off catching of
the sunlight, in drawing or painting. The songs are
extremely vivid, as fresh as dawn, and always suggestive.
What if they are a little rough and unshaven, a little slap-
dash in technique, a little undistinguished in their actual
texture? Their appeal is direct, uninterrupted between
composer and auditor provided the singer is sensible and
does not intrude himself unnecessarily. They are music for
a Prom audience, and make no other pretensions. R.L.S.
had a curious *panache* about him; however deeply felt, his
verses share something with the characters of his fiction.
And this almost-swagger Vaughan Williams reproduces
with a slight and rather youthful self-consciousness.

"The Vagabond," which opens Book I, is the most complete work of art of all the seven songs. One dares to wonder
how R.L.S. himself would have liked it, for the verses bear
the superscription, "To an air by Schubert." The spare
texture is kept interesting not only by the marching figure,
but also by an original and entirely logical harmonic scheme.
"Bright is the Ring of Words" is less distinctive: indeed, it
has no more distinction than, for example, the setting of the
same words by W. H. Hadow, who, great man though he
was, as a composer had no pretensions to be more than a
dilettante. The scheme of development, varying the two
strophes, is not entirely happy; the rhythmic treatment of
the words is its best point. "The Roadside Fire," for all its
charm, hardly escapes the charge of clumsiness; and the
lengthening of the basic pulse in the last verse does not help.
Comparison can be made with Peter Warlock's setting,
called "Romance," an early and little-known song of his
(1919) which has much more of the cockade, the feather in
the hat, the jauntiness, of the words, and is, in its way, a
technically perfect miniature.

Book II of *Songs of Travel* shows more miscellaneity of
styles. In the romantic "Let Beauty Awake" we are back
in the Rossetti phase, whereas "Youth and Love" takes us
far on into later works: the latter is a sketch for many things

that occur in *On Wenlock Edge* and in *Hugh the Drover* and even in *Sancta Civitas*. One does not know how much of Hugo Wolf Vaughan Williams had heard by 1907, but there is certainly an affinity in the style of the next song, "In Dreams Unhappy." The texture is purely harmonic, and does not inspire in one the feeling of certainty. "The Infinite Shining Heavens," on the other hand, is vocal declamation over the stillest and faintest of backgrounds, and here again we "look in the dusk," as Stevenson did, and see the star come down in many of the more philosophical passages in later works. The open spaces are cosmic.

Two other songs of this period require passing mention here; the first, a setting of Shakespeare's *Orpheus with his Lute*, because some thirty years later the composer made another setting which is as mature and simple as this early one is jejune. The other is *Linden Lea*, music set to a Dorsetshire-dialect poem of William Barnes, which after the turn of the nineteen-twenties came in for a sudden and quite unexpected vogue. A more fitting music (original, not an adaptation) could not be found for this charming poem. It is, indeed, an example of "Bright is the ring of words when the right man rings them, Fair the fall of songs when the singer sings them"; for the composer seems to be uttering words and music together out of his own heart, as if both were his creation. The style is that of the English countryside, and brings to mind the note in the preface to the opera *Sir John in Love*, where the composer, explaining his use of folk-song therein, writes: "When I could not find a suitable folk-tune, I have made shift to make up something of my own." In *Linden Lea* the shift led to the right song.

In the same year as the publishing of *Songs of Travel*, Book II, occurs an event of considerable importance in Vaughan Williams's life as a composer. The 1907 Leeds Festival gave the first performance of his *Toward the Unknown Region*, described by the composer as a "song for chorus and orchestra."

Biographically the performance is significant enough, for

its success opened the door for Vaughan Williams to enter
the world of the English Festivals in the North and West
country, with which he has never lost connexion. Oppor-
tunities for hearing new major works by living English composers were rarer then than even now, and the Festivals thus
provided composers with an outlet. As I have hinted before,
the predominance of choral writing in Vaughan Williams's
early works was only partly due to a natural predilection for
the voice and its words, but also attributable to greater
chances of audition.

Musically *Toward the Unknown Region* has an even greater
significance. Plunket Greene, who was singing at that
Festival, describes it as "new in its outlook, and new in its
working out, and enthralling in its beautiful interpretation of
the words." The three points are well chosen. English
music had not produced a massive and broad and bare choral
style like this one since the days of Purcell, save in the work
of the imported Handel. There is a new, and for this composer an unprecedented, firmness of handling of the
material. And, thirdly, it is indeed a song, a choral song,
but not the less an expression of words by the singing voice.

The literary background of Vaughan Williams's imagination has changed. Walt Whitman's verse has had a liberating
effect upon him. After Stevenson's rather carefully placed,
nostalgic words, after Rossetti's bowed head and stained-
glass attitudes, this poem is positively gusty in its open-air-
ness. The unknown region is no dark corner of a cellar or a
hothouse. "There's a wind on the heath, Life is very sweet,
brother," and there is "no map there, nor guide, nor touch
of human hand"; we come in this music to the moment
when we all can join in with the chorus's words, "Then we
burst forth, we float, in time and space." In fact, we burst
forth very successfully, but float a little to excess, in our
desire to be "equal, equipt at last."

What matter if "Love's Last Gift" and *Toward the
Unknown Region* have an almost identical melody, even to
the immediate repetition in the mediant major? The whole

musical intention has altered under the expansive, aspiring influence of Whitman. We meet "uplift" (which the *Concise Oxford Dictionary* defines as "chiefly U.S.A.—elevating influence"). I cannot go hand in hand with Dr Colles in *Grove* and many others who write of Whitman's "rugged" verse. His words are perhaps rugged, but his philosophy was woolly at the edges. Let me concede that his verse has jagged edges softened to sight by mist.

The democratic aim was something new in English music. Here, probably for the first time in our 'serious' music, outside the Church, was a body of people banded together to praise the liberation of the soul. The work demands of the choir something more than vocal skill and power: it demands community of spirit, a get-together-ness, a combined resolution to explore "that region, that inaccessible land." That spirit of seeking, of freedom sought and won, was no new spirit in English poetry, any more than it was in English social life. Music tends always to lag behind the visual, poetic, and dramatic arts. *Toward the Unknown Region* calls up as clearly as thoughts of the Mermaid Tavern the "souls of poets dead and gone." In no sense does it decry Whitman to find in Vaughan Williams's music reminders of Shelley, of Browning, of Malthus and Tom Paine and Charles Darwin, of the Fabians, and of that movement which was growing to its climax of violence about the time of its composition and the following years—the Suffragist movement. No one had in England successfully applied to music this seething undercurrent of desire for liberation of soul until he gave the Leeds Choir this music to sing in 1907. I do not pretend to be able to assess the spiritual quality of *Toward the Unknown Region*: such moral values must be left to others. I am certain, however, that it leads us to a greater spaciousness of mind, and if the "wide open spaces" are ill-defined in their delimitations, any choir will be able to sing the music with the fervour of "truly exploring," even if it is only the exploration of new avenues of mind from the sedentary safety of the office chair. Already the native accent can be heard in the musical speech. Dr Harry Colles, in the birthday-leader ın *The Times* of October 12, 1942, wrote that we call this music of Vaughan Williams's English

> because at one moment the style may recall an English folk-song, at another the polyphony of Tallis or Byrd, or the rich freedom of Purcell's declamation in song; but musical ancestry does not explain the unity. How many composers of all nations have been hampered in the expression of themselves by the consciousness of their ancestry? Nationality has been a snare because it has been a garment self-consciously worn, not a formative influence on personal character.

In form the 'song' (or cantata) is curiously lyrical, despite the large forces used and the looseness of the rhythm of the stanzas. A melody mentioned before first appears in many forms, all of them full of questioning—"Darest thou now, O soul, walk out with me toward the unknown region?" The music is bare. "No map there" gives us a semitone drop which is a Vaughan Williams characteristic. (*Cf. A Sea Symphony* and the D major Symphony, first movement: it is one of his ways of shadowing in the mysterious and undefined, and has no relation that I can see with the celebrated phrase in Beethoven's Violin Concerto.) A third vocal phrase ("no touch of human hand") follows in concert with a counterpoint of the same notes in diminution (is it really effective?). That is all the material. The rest is development and a final 'bursting forth'; the questioning first phrase is now removed from all puzzles and doubts. The long song of the choir is immensely effective, and only praise is meant by my comment that the part-writing relies more on the singers' lungs than upon rule-of-thumb. An expressional *tour de force*, it all sounds far better than it reads: which is what good music, especially choral music, always does.

The next Leeds Festival, three years later than that which produced the *Unknown Region*, introduced to the public (1910) *A Sea Symphony*. Not only date-order but every other logical conclusion would offer to lead us from the foothills of the *Unknown Region* to the *Sea Symphony*'s spacious atmosphere and wider views. Yet it is recorded that the first thoughts of the second choral work occurred as early as 1903, pre-dating the first by a considerable period. The Walt Whitman phase takes root in *Leaves of Grass*, it seems, and it would thus appear that the *Unknown Region* grew out of the *Sea Symphony*, and not the other way round —a paradoxical situation not without parallel in the development of this apparently unparadoxical composer. Regarded as a practical experiment in the musical setting of Whitman's words, as a model for a more composite group of statuary, *Toward the Unknown Region* reflects a light which was only dimly visible to audience and critics forty years ago. We can look at it to-day not as the starting-point of the journey, but rather as a marking-buoy on the broad ocean voyage which was to become the *Sea Symphony*.

A Sea Symphony begins and ends as a song, and as a song it is huge. As a symphony it shrinks in dimensions, belittled by its musical and technical immaturities. What selfless outpouring of voice it demands! Every square inch of lung, every foot-pound of diaphragm pressure, will hardly suffice. The conscious liberalist "uplift" of the daring quest for the Unknown Region has been transformed into "a song for all seas, all ships," "spiritual woven signal for all nations, emblem of man elate above death," which produces a cataract of music showering over us, poured with enormous energy by the choristers. The wide generalities of Whitman are given "a local habitation and a name" in the music. They are not hemmed in, but spilt from the intellectual stratosphere to a terrestrial ocean.

Two English choral works so diametrically opposite as Vaughan Williams's *Sea Symphony* and Delius's *Sea Drift* could hardly be found, despite the links of Walt Whitman's poetry and the word 'sea' in the titles. Delius, in his piece, is the subjective mood-painter, the anthropomorphic dreamer about the brown birds; impressionistic in style, subtle and accomplished in technical expression, nostalgic, musing on memories, touched emotionally more by what is not there than by what is. He broods in an exquisite musical rhapsody. Vaughan Williams, on the other hand, is obsessed with the presence of the water: his basic fact is the sea, ceaseless, moving at his feet. He views the sea as a landsman, an islander to whom the coast offers the one exit towards exploration. Though in his music he expresses the far view of the merchant adventurer, he never seems to be in mid-ocean. His horizon is measured from the shore—wide enough, indeed, but without the loneliness of the full Atlantic. His is the spectator's point of view, the outlook of a typical scion of a sea-going insular race. We are *en plein air*, buffeted by the weather out of introspection, breathless a little, with no time to waste, even "on the beach at night alone," for reminiscent dreams. But we are on land. The technique is not only less accomplished than that of Delius, but intentionally rougher, as suits the boat-builder's carpentry of the words.

There can be no doubt, I think, about the stature of the *Sea Symphony*, of its success as an achievement (public and artistic), nor of its vigour, its many moments of enduring beauty, its firmness of style. Such weaknesses as it displays are quite other than those Parry saw. We should not expect to reach the summit early in this composer's rising walk towards the uplands of music. He takes us, so soon, to an altitude or a tide-mark where we can catch the wind on our faces.

If in 1907 Vaughan Williams opened the windows upon the stuffy chambers of the outworn Victorian tradition of English choral music, in 1910 he laid it bare to the four winds of heaven, with Whitman adding the energy of human directive force to the natural ebullience of the sea air. *A Sea Symphony* is a moderately mature work; it manifests an increase of power, a breadth of expression, a management of the medium, and a sureness of touch not to be seen in any previous work by the composer. The scale is large, and there is a flood of musical invention. The prophets of 1910 were justified in their recognition that there had arrived at Leeds an important English composer, of the true metal and proper weight. Hubert Parry wrote in a letter of 1914: "A very good performance of Vaughan Williams's *Sea Symphony*. Big stuff, but full of impertinences as well as noble moments." One wonders exactly what impertinences; for to our ears the influence of Parry himself, as a focus of the English choral tradition, is strongly noticeable. Was it in part, perhaps, the opening harmonic figure, in part the mixture of diatonic and modal harmony, in part the sheer picturesqueness of some sections? I do not underrate the originality of the work, nor forget the changes in taste of forty years, when I say that to-day we find *A Sea Symphony* safe and comfortable in idiom, disturbing only in the gusty vigour of its spirit.

When, "forty years on," one experiences the work again in the shock of aural perception, one is conscious of its magnitude—though it is, one finds, larger in conception than in achievement. The impertinences have faded away like forgotten slang, and the musical effect is, each time anew, one of unquenchable freshness. The audience leaves the hall mentally drenched with salt spray. For myself, I consider that the main weaknesses arise from the words. Just as they were the composer's source of inspiration, so in the end they became his handicap, his fetters. The mind flew away on the winds of symphonic development, the words tugged at the string of the kite; the result is some audible fluttering. The admirable choral treatment is massive, in block formation, and no one is the worse if the poet's lines are repeated, or in any other way inaudible. But with the soloists it is a different matter. Some of the phrases they have to sing are unsusceptible. "A pennant universal" is not emphatic in music, and few singers would choose to enounce "Thou actual me," or "But to you reserve especially for yourself . . . one half above all the rest." Balance of choir and soloists is imperfect because of the alphabetic barriers, which dam the symphonic flow. The scoring is unsympathetic to the awkward registers of soprano and

baritone.[1] Wagnerean influence has been overrated; anything less like Bayreuth is inconceivable. Through all the
immature difficulties the inspiration shines with a bright
light, untarnished by the years. The work stands, as English
as our climate.

A strong English character appears, unformed maybe but
clear. As Colles wrote:

> It is character that has made Vaughan Williams's compositions
> what they are. His music declares a character lovable by the
> simple-minded, baffling to the sophisticated. Eager propagandists
> who made a cause of the advancement of the art either for its own
> sake or for some immediate social benefit are at a loss where to place
> him. He has avoided official recognition, sometimes a little wilfully,
> it has seemed; he has refused to write for special occasions. Yet
> when a King comes to be crowned or an Archbishop to be enthroned,
> there is the *Te Deum* or the motet apt for the purpose, though
> neither is concerned with the pageantry of the occasion. He looks
> beyond. "O farther, farther sail," and "Towards the unknown
> region" are salient texts from the American poet in whose "rude,
> brief recitative" he has found congenial companionship.[2]

Due consideration of *A Sea Symphony* as the first-born of
a family of six is given in the next chapter. Some discussion
of technique may come timely here, as throwing light upon
Vaughan Williams's musical method.

The spacing of the words in the first movement is interesting. Of the twenty-eight lines (of varying length) of the
poem the first twenty-three occupy twenty-five pages of
vocal score, the remaining five, twenty-one. Despite the
swinging and spacious movement of the first main subject,
the "song for all ships" depends for its solidity of construction on the memorable tune invented for the words "token
of all brave captains," first introduced as a striding bass
under ejaculatory chorus, and developed with energy and
concentration from bar 17 to bar 25. We have met that

---

[1] I once heard a performance with two unduly eminent soloists, neither of whom
was audible, which reminded me of the old party trick of reproducing a speech as
seen, but not heard, by some one sitting on the skylight above the speaker.
[2] *The Times*, October 12, 1942, in the leader already quoted.

triplet before, in the *Unknown Region*. Much has been written about the boldness of the harmonic progression of the opening—B flat minor to D major. Is it in truth so bold? It appears in one form or another in the Rossetti period, in the *Pastoral Symphony*, and elsewhere. As a fingerprint, a prelude to what is in store for us, those chords are impressive. The whole first part is narrative in style. The modal melisma of the "rude, brief recitative" is used dramatically in various developments in subsequent movements. The "chant for the sailors of all nations" is a fine, open tune, subjected to what I feel to be rather uncomfortable harmonic development. In fact, we are meant to remain in a state of suspense till the soprano reaches her declamatory top A and leads us to a new and more taut mood.

Vaughan Williams has suddenly turned away from contemplation of "the sea itself," towards the "intrepid sailors and mates": the ocean becomes peopled not only with ships, but with fellow-men, and with their individual and collective struggles to master the elements and their lives. The effect on the musical manner is marked. Here, if anywhere, is the English tradition:

> Hark, a song
>   Marvellously welling
> From the first song
>   Of poets praising ladies
> English and dear,
>   Broke over us there:
> Hark, their voices rang
>   As we sat, as we smiled,
> Hark, their music rang,
>   Young and fresh and wild,
> Tossed on the London light:
>   Lovelace, Sackville, and Carew,
> All were singing, and we too,
>   "Good-night to all you ladies,
> Good-night!"[1]

---

[1] "The English Tradition," from *Windows of Night*, by Charles Williams (Clarendon Press, 1924).

Those words were written about a London omnibus. Musicans might wish, perhaps, to substitute the names of Gibbons and Weelkes, Byrd and Purcell and Blow, for those Charles Williams thought of. And yet, much though he is indebted to the choralists, Vaughan Williams has close affinity with "Lovelace, Sackville, and Carew." Without secularizing the English Church tradition he has enlarged the religious scope from music designed for worship to a broad humanitarianism, all-embracing and strong in its sympathy.

The texture is at first contrapuntal, the melodic interest of high importance, with harmony relying for its own interest much on the suspension and the secondary seventh. After the first carefully built choral climax the treatment becomes more symphonic in style, and leads to a kind of stretto (compare the last movement of the D major Symphony) which adds a massive tower to the whole.

From here onward there is a reversion to the vaguer and more rhetorical style of the opening movement. But Whitman's verses are vaguely rhetorical, and so thanks may be offered that the music is as firm as even this! The coda uses a rich pentatonic texture, with the voices dying out into nothing.

For some the second movement ("On the beach at night alone") is a favourite. I cannot share this personal preference. The picture is well painted as a study in mood. The words are set with good realization—apart from the accentuations of the soloist. We find, somehow, in our watch on the veiled sea, that "vast similitude." (I have found it a "humilitude" —as Stevenson's Will o' the Mill says, "We are in a rat-trap.") The colouring is suitably imposing in its indigo shades; there is utter solemnity, until, for a short spell, there is a reminder of the others in the "all nations." The movement ends darkly, with the mother crooning again, on a Whitmanesque note of hope in the G sharps.

Alone the movement does not stand firmly on its feet. As a part of a bigger work, despite quotation from the past and a leading on to the future, the music has its place. But it is, as music, too picturesque. Impressive and mysterious, the sounds bring with them that curious static pictorialism of the magic lantern. The hearer is, by intention, looking at 'views.'

On the other hand, the scherzo, following so closely as to tread on the heels of the rapt, watching figure, affects me in the opposite way. Here is no set piece. The composer is tossed about by his imagination as if his ideas were waves themselves. The clumsiness is the rough-and-tumble of surf-bathing. We are left glowing and wet: the wind will dry us, never fear! A spacious tune ("Where the great vessel sailing") provides the fine dignity of a seafaring history: every one ought to join in, in unison, on the top line, standing up to raise voices to the sky.

The "vast rondure, swimming in space" is suggested, in all its incomprehensibility, by the first six bars of the fourth and last movement. In the seventh bar comes a tenor lead in the chorus which bears out the view that the words hold back the firm progress of this symphony. It is matter for debate; but one can hardly consider the tenor's lead vocally effective. He has to sing an instrumental phrase, beyond the right power of human emphasis.

The ensuing bars are led away by Whitman's philo-sophizing. Suddenly (at p. 85 of the vocal score) the music comes to life. After some string chords (a little reminiscent of Coleridge-Taylor, perhaps?) a Dorian mode tells us about Adam and Eve, with real mystery, which works up splendidly to "that sad incessant refrain"

> Wherefore unsatisfied soul,
> Whither, O mocking life?

The voices sing in *oratio obliqua*, as in the Rossetti works: a female semi-chorus asks the question. For a moment the universe stands still. The echo is equally immobile and remote: we are transported to Stevenson's "infinite shining heavens": the music moves on, skilfully, to a rather incon-

G

gruously Parryish climax. Then the soloists burst in—they
"can wait no longer."

Long years of love for this noble piece stand behind me,
barring critical judgement. Perhaps love is the proper
emotion with which to brave its onslaughts of spray and
undisciplined rollers. I will obey the pentatonic last injunc-
tion, and will "farther sail."

Despite his first big success, his coming to man's estate
as a composer at the age of thirty-eight, Vaughan Williams's
mind was not, in the 1910 period, occupied wholly by the
aspiring idiom of the *Sea Symphony*. English as it is to the
bone, that work bears little more trace of folk-song influence
than the use of the Dorian mode of Adam and Eve descending
from the Garden of Eden. Yet, apart from his work on *The
English Hymnal* and the *Norfolk Rhapsodies*, Vaughan
Williams was making excursions into folk-music arrangement. There are the *Five English Folk-songs* and the
Fantasia on Christmas Carols for baritone solo, chorus, and
orchestra.

Evidence of Englishry had been given at Leeds and other
public places indirectly. Here we meet the people's words
and music but little altered for musicans to sing and play to
the audience.

The group of "*Five English Folk-songs*, freely arranged
for unaccompanied chorus," and dated 1913, make up a
curiously complete work. Each number is, of course,
entirely separate and unrelated, and comes from an individual
source. Moods are well contrasted, Nos. 1 and 3 being
stirring narrative songs of great jollity, No. 5 a kind of
communal, almost professional climax, and Nos. 2 and 4
slow, emotional songs. The choral treatment is moderately
elaborate: the music demands skill and willingness in performance. At the same time the songs always give enjoyment
to keen singers, and a very good tonal effect can be continuously produced by those who have more enthusiasm and
musical interest than adroitness. A 'crack' Welsh Eisteddfod

choir might easily make nothing of this music, while a scratch body of music students could 'bring them off' with care. As compositions they show both skill and imagination. Especially, we are given the full value of the folk-songs. The art of the arranger is such that we notice very little of him and yet receive a complete and rich imaginative version of the original tunes. Exposition is already masterly. Of the influence of these arrangements on choral taste and other composers no firm judgement can be formed. Some inner sense leads me to believe it was enormous.

Less firmly handled is the *Fantasia on Christmas Carols*, for baritone solo, chorus, and orchestra (1912). This is no more than a *quodlibet*—a string of Christmas tunes picked at the composer's will to fit into some sort of pattern. (*A Christmas Carol* is another.) The work has a considerable if rather domestic charm, even though it has the air of being a little uncomfortable in its fine clothes. As a sketch for later pieces, almost an exercise, the *Fantasia* bears study, and it is pleasant to hear.

Given over to composing, Vaughan Williams's mind had also time, at this period, to consider the English composer in relation to the English musical habits of life, and enjoyment, and education. At pp. 197–201 of this book may be read his essay on "Who wants the British Composer?" published in the *R.C.M. Magazine* in 1912. The journal would seem to be too restricted in its circulation, in its special appeal, for the wide-spreading doctrines he preached, outspokenly and for the first time in our later history. But, though many years have marked the entrance of a new era, the reader will find that what he wrote so long ago has grave pertinence to-day—both in its general thesis and in the application of that thesis to practical details of composing.

Three more cycles of songs take prominent place in the early period: fifteen songs in all. *On Wenlock Edge* (for tenor voice and piano quintet) was first sung in London on November 15, 1909, by Gervase Elwes. The *Five Mystical*

Songs, for baritone solo, chorus (*ad. lib.*), and orchestra, were first given at the Three Choirs' Festival at Worcester in 1911, the soloist being Campbell McInnes. The work is available also for solo voice and piano, and is more frequently heard in this form. The *Four Hymns*, for tenor voice, viola obbligato, and strings, written in 1914, had to wait for performance till the Worcester Festival of 1920. Of the three works, *On Wenlock Edge* is the most familiar to the public, partly because of its romantic association with Gervase Elwes, partly because it was the first major work written after the composer's short sojourn with Ravel, and no doubt for "many other reasons why."

The three works together show how many-pathed was the exploratory course followed by this adventurous musical mind. The Housman songs stand in isolation; the two other cycles, though they both draw on the metaphysical poets (including Bridges) for their words, are different in their styles in a subtle but noticeable way. Each of the cycles is conceived as a whole; not one of the songs therein is designed to be heard as a separate work. At the time under consideration Vaughan Williams's mind was occupied with extended forms, with large canvases and broad designs. He remains the same to this day, more interested in the wide spiritual issue than the details of expression. He is the last composer to call a miniaturist.

English song in the 1900–10 period was only beginning to rouse itself from two centuries of torpor. Harry Plunket Greene, pioneer in the performance of good songs set to intelligible words, has summed up the matter in a vivid picture (even his pen had a touch of Irish accent). Though he was writing of a time rather earlier than that of Vaughan Williams's cycles, so much of what he wrote applies to the latter that he is worth quoting *in extenso*.

"Song at that time," wrote Plunket Greene,

was in a transition stage. Professional singing was still going round in circles in its own back eddy, with oratorio and the "royalty" ballad taking their turns in the wash. Lieder singing was mostly in the hands of the amateur and being looked on as "precious" was therefore suspect. It was not until George Henschel got into his stride that it began to take hold. He, not being British-born, was granted a good-natured licence to sing what he liked, and it was not long till his genius captured the public. But, though neither he nor they knew it, he was a product of the new time. A new generation had come to birth which looked into the future and loved its mother tongue. Cambridge had seen it stir and helped it from its chrysalis. Imagination had come again to British music. Purcell's lone star was shining through the clouds again, and the Elizabethans were moving in their graves.

Looking at it in perspective it is possible to trace the hand of Providence in the British musical renaissance. Mackenzie was born in 1847, Parry in 1848, and Stanford in 1852. These three broke away from the borrowed Handel-Mendelssohn tradition and started, quite unconsciously, the imaginative school of composition. Then came Mary Wakefield, who, again unwittingly, founded the Competition Festival Movement which has spread throughout the Empire. Then Cecil Sharp arrived and saved our folk-songs and folk-dances for us in the nick of time; and finally came Edmund Fellowes who restored and edited our famous Elizabethans and completed the magic circle.

Only the long sight of history can make this clear. The modern eye is too bloodshot still to wish to see. Internal-combustion engines, mechanization, the harnessing of the ether and bloody war have overrun the intelligence like a flood, and in that spate all that went before is so much common flotsam. Maybe one day long hence when Time has taken a breathing-spell, some searcher in the British Museum may come across *The Woman of Samaria* and *The May Queen*, and, close beside, *The Glories of our Blood and State* and *The Revenge*, and wonder what had happened in between.

The revolution was not one of method. There was no conscious breaking away from tradition harmonically, or contrapuntally, or from foundations in general. It was a matter of imagination, which blew in like a fresh wind from the sea. They had fresh things to say, and fresh ways to say them, and a spirit of adventure which laughed at conventions.[1]

Flung with an almost petulant vigour into the middle of the post-Victorian period, *On Wenlock Edge* must have

[1] *Charles Villiers Stanford* (Arnold, 1935).

caused considerable surprise. The songs differed from both
Parry's and Stanford's almost as much as *A Sea Symphony*
differed from Delius. The complacency of those long years
of peace and prosperity, industrial revolution and social
reform, all managed on 'high moral grounds'—that very
complacency which has caused the later thirty years' war—
was not then ready to be disturbed. There is no record of
what Parry thought of the song-cycle: but it certainly has
ten "impertinences" for every one in the earlier Symphony.
From the very opening the third degree of the common chord
is roughly elbowed out of the way by a tonic of two superimposed fourths; the semitone is avoided with some con-
scientiousness; even the peaceful A major scale at the end of
"Clun" has a D sharp. It is perhaps not surprising, though
not excusable, that the charge was made against the composer that he was here influenced by Ravel. If the Frenchman had any influence at all, he made Vaughan Williams
realize that he was not a Frenchman, might have been a
Prussian, but remained an Englishman. The cycle splashed
into our musical stream, muddy as it was with the tributaries
of Brahms and Dvořák and the ebbing trickles of Mendelssohn, Schumann, and Spohr, as a bather, a very simple
English countryman, naked and unashamed, in his own
stream.

A. E. Housman's slender volume of 1896, *A Shropshire
Lad*, was at the time an interesting and original source of
poetry for music. Only Butterworth had then turned to it.
Later, Housman attained the dubious honour of being the
most frequently set-to-music of the poets of the early
twentieth century. Like another poet of similar date, W. B.
Yeats, he was sublimely unconcerned with music. His
letters show that he was incapable of understanding the urge
his words gave to musicians, and that he was unwilling to
accept Wagner's idea that poetry fertilizes music. We must
guess to-day what had happened in the growing mind of
Vaughan Williams to cause him to switch suddenly from the
nebulous upliftings of Walt Whitman, the search for the

brotherhood of man in the clouds and in the animals, to what Charles Williams properly calls "such catastrophic despair" in Housman. I continue with words from Charles Williams's *Poetry at Present*[1]:

> When Mr Housman wrote the lines
>
> > Therefore, since the world has still
> > Much good, but much less good than ill
>
> he recorded not only his own but also Hardy's vision of this world. . . . But the temper with which his [Housman's] verse has expressed that vision, continuously and epigrammatically, is very different from Hardy's. The revolt and distress which exist in the older poet's work are not to be found. . . . Mr Housman has invented no God to blame.

A composer's desire for English epigram after Whitman's American imageries is one thing; an acceptance of Housman's deliberate and depressing godlessness is quite another. It consorts ill with the firm if imaginative faith of the metaphysicals; and, indeed, it can only be explained on literary grounds. "There have been cries of romantic personal despair, but this verse is classic in its restraint and calm balance." We must look to Housman's polished manner of using the English language if we would understand Vaughan Williams's choice of poet at the same time that he was thinking also of the *Five Mystical Songs*.

How far the music of the *Wenlock Edge* cycle is in proportion with the quiet, subtle, speech-order verses of *Shropshire Lad* Housman is matter for opinion. Many other composers have produced, since 1909, music more carefully designed as settings for these "jewels five words long," more exactly balanced musical counterparts to the poet's self-conscious simplicity. But no composer has yet produced a cycle to these words which enlarges their inner human meaning to so extensive a symphonic scale. There are moments when a piano quintet and a single voice seem a slender medium for the musical ideas. Horns one can hear, a chorus, clarinets

[1] Clarendon Press, 1930.

holding dotted minims—and yet the orchestral transcription is less successful than the original scoring.

The work is rough-hewn, a carving of figures made from an unpolished, solid tree-trunk, with only the bark skimmed off. There are difficulties that become apparent in rehearsal; yet the performance reveals an unforgettable beauty not to be gauged by a reading of the score. In part this practical loveliness is due to the free speech-rhythm of the voice, which has to be understandingly followed by the instrumentalists (for whom body rhythm is a more common medium). *On Wenlock Edge* is, above all, an original work; I would claim for it an originality no less important in musical history, only less spectacular and less international, than that of Debussy's *Images*.

In the first song the voice strongly declaims the words, and the instruments are concerned with the atmospheric effects of "the gale that plies the saplings double," which seems to be more important than the poet's vision of the Roman, now "ashes under Uricon," who (like the singer) watched the same gale in back years. The whole implies a pantheistic faith that is beyond Housman. The musical idiom is a curious mixture of bare fourths and picturesque chromatic melismas. "From far, from Eve and Morning," the second song, keeps closer to the poet's track of thought: the second stanza, with its free, urgent speech, reproduces the restrained but tragic passion that underlies Housman. The spread chords at the opening and end are a familiar part of Vaughan Williams's style, to be found as early as the Rossetti songs and as late as the slow movement of the D major Symphony. Nos. 3 and 5 are narrative songs; in the earlier the words are consciously reminiscent of the ballad, in the latter less so, at once more purely poetic and more oddly colloquial. The composer characterizes the dead lad and the living clearly and swiftly, the ghost by a distant-sounding modal figure, the survivor by a descending chromatic passage on the 'cello. Drama is compressed to an intensity that is almost unbearable. "Bredon Hill" extends the dramatic range until it

strains the medium, with the deliberate jangle of distant bells
as a continuing and developed background: "the coloured
counties" are so close, so important, that they dwarf the
human figures in the foreground. An influence of unaccompanied folk-singing is felt, without any definite marks, in the
vocal line, which, wayward throughout, at the climax is bid
go on "irrespective" of the accompaniment. The song is a
tour de force of impressionistic painting, but classifies itself
rather as a *scena* than as a lyrical utterance. Between the two
story-telling songs comes a moment of light relief—one of
the poet's more cynical epigrams, fitted suitably by the
composer to a parody of English folk-song. "Oh, when I
was in love with you" is not separable from the cycle; no
singer would sing it alone.

The sixth and last movement of the work is, considered
as a song, the most satisfying work of art, and has the most
haunting music. Housman's words in "Clun" are human,
but they are not religious. That nothingness of the grave
which the poet offers the composer colours with a certain
ray of hope. Those lads who "had trouble at Knighton"
give him apparently an untroubled view of their future. The
musical flow has the proper geographical steadiness for "the
country of easy livers, the quietest under the sun." A
dropping phrase speaks of eternity to me. And then comes
a splendid tune! *Forty-ninth Parallel* has another: but these
two are not his first nor his last melodies. A moment is
created, and I am constrained, out of love (not Whitman's
'love' nor Rossetti's), to sing it silently to myself. I stand in
reverence, for this love is equally hopeful and despairing.

The cycle, as a whole, may be criticized as 'sketchy.' But
the lines of the sketcher are bold, done with the hand of a
Vinci or a John. Those convincing, bold lines, that no one
else would think of, Vaughan Williams broadly draws. His
determinate mind seeks the landing rather than one step on
the stair. If he stumbles over a tread or a riser, he arrives
safely at the top storey.

A wide gulf divides Whitman from Housman, a lesser

(but adventurous) gulf Housman from Herbert. The slender bridge of colloquial talk makes the supporting struts of Herbert seem rusty by Housman's time. The latter uses a people's language, the former the literary tongue of a 'class.' In the *Five Mystical Songs* our Christian God appears in a religion which is uninstitutional: in a faith that accepts no local tradition, but only the Christian Church as England once saw it; a faith prone to pantheism rather than to conservatism of forms; a faith that might find in the external aspects of the Cathedral an inspiration, but would have little traffic with its later conventions. The *Five Mystical Songs*, in a phrase, give us the English faith without the trammels of weekly parish usage: they express the creed without the need for Dean and Chapter.

George Herbert (1593–1633), cadet of the family of Edward, first Lord Herbert of Cherbury, wore a courtly air. Reading those of Herbert's words which Vaughan Williams set—reading them again in the frigidity of poetic print, critically and without warmer memory—I find the fantastic comes to my reading brain as simple, imaginative, and exquisite; I find no savour of the euphuistic in the lines:

> The Sun arising in the East
>> Though he give light, and the East perfume;
> If they should offer to contest,
>> With thy arising, they presume.

"They" means the flowers he brought "to strew thy way"; are "they" more phantasmal than those impersonals, "the singing masons building roofs of gold," or the "they" of T. S. Eliot's cat poems; "when they reach the scene of crime —*Macavity's not there*!" I see the flowers in my little strip of garden.

Extravagances or no, Vaughan Williams manages the words with a new musical ease. They seem to suit him. The early *Fantasy Quintet* would show that his style at this period was earth-bound, and, indeed, he treats Herbert with the literalness he gives to the hymn-writers in *The English Hymnal*. Not all the poems are handled in the same manner, yet they form a body of five limbs only to be separated by surgical treatment. The idioms are exploratory and varied, as in the Symphonies.

"Easter," first of the five, opens with the words "Rise, heart, the Lord is risen." The musical command to the heart to rise, in that opening fourth from B flat to E flat, has awoken me on many occasions from the indolence induced by modern conditions of life, but on others I have wondered whether the rest of the phrase gives us Herbert's vision. The tonal manner is disguised by Wesley's secondary sevenths, which come from Bach. Quieter moments recall to us "emotion remembered in tranquillity." Are these quiet moments better than those of command? There is a tang of the Rossetti manner in the middle, but the new accomplishment of technical skill offers us a rich acoustic pattern.

"There is but one, and that one ever"; the words turn us from America and the Welsh marches to an endeavour, by the composer, to square the circle of life, or to spiralize the square. The harmonic problem of consecutive fifths and octaves is posed, with an obvious change of philosophic passion. We have left the secondary sevenths, and turn in this second song to harmonized plainsong, to harmonized melisma, with variations.

"Love bade me Welcome," the third, is a talkative piece, in style expository, but neither modal nor tonal. "Welcome," we are called by "quick-eyed love"; and we may already accept, not waiting for the fifth in order of the Symphonies to reach peace of acceptance. We can find the mystical humility and faith of the poet. Our troubles are solved in the major tonality of "O Sacrum Convivium," and though the words "go slack," when this other love "took my hand," we bridge the years in hopefulness.

The hymn which is the fourth song is an act of private, not public, worship; a hymn sung by one man in a cloister, a prayer with a personal melody. Few acknowledged composers, living beyond the pale of the monastery, could so clearly, carefully, and religiously expound the meaning of these verses. Extravagant? Fantastic? I think not!

"Antiphon" bursts out with clatter: *risoluto* and *non legato*. The directions should not be needed by singers who understand music. The scale-figure, the successive fourths, the wind-swept tune, should force us, "all the world in every corner," to sing. With resonant bareness God is praised in a new sonority. Perhaps this "Osanna" heralds the coming of a modern English Bach.

The *Four Hymns* have not outwardly the vigorous public appeal of the Herbert set of five. Yet they mark an intellectual advance on their predecessor, and show, as a treatment of metaphysical words, a musical progress. The fourth, to Robert Bridges's words, translated into real English verse from the Greek Anthology, is the most interesting from the technical point of view in music (see pp. 74–75). Here is a pattern, given to us in poise and yet curiously unmechanical in its methods. The contrapuntal cross-rhythms may not quite fit; the words are beautifully placed, against the instruments, in emphatic climax. A lovely song, it holds a big place in the procession of Vaughan Williams's thoughts. "Lord, come away!" (the first song) is a cutting from the Purcell root—what a Purcell sprig ought to have flowered into in our twentieth century. "Hosanna" (though it recalls Purcell) is heated to a white temperature unthought of musically in Purcell's day. No. 2 is a narrative song, in which the singer's accentuation must not be tripped up by cross-accents. The Crashaw setting (No. 3) is a little more mannered, as the poet was, and may be a little obscure to the hearer.

Different though the nine songs are in style, they coalesce into one piece of thought—one long dream. Yet of the nine-fold musing, the later four manifest a new passion, something beyond Herbert, without his range because they derive their origin from his way of thought and have re-created it in a later age. We are romantically hot to-day; uncomfortable,

and subjected to introspective furies; but as post-romantics
we are finally convinced.

To the technical inquirer into idiom I recommend a
study of the cadences; they lead, not to finality, but to a
new enlightenment. Every avoidance of tonic and dominant
is sought by the composer—the flattened seventh, the modal
variants, the Bach rising bass, the Purcellian moving bass,
strange (but understandable) chordal progressions—all these
draw us on to an appreciation of a new beauty that exists
only in the music and will not be synthesized by my words.

The first harvesting of orchestral music in Vaughan
Williams's musical life yields a less fruitful crop than that
in the adjacent vocal field. Five pieces survive from the
period that closes with 1914, excluding the *London Symphony*, which, though written at this time and first played in
that year, did not reach final form until after the First World
War.

One remembers, as one looks back, Samuel Butler's
remark that "Life is like playing a violin solo in public and
learning the instrument as one goes on." Another entry in
Butler's *Notebooks* says: "Life is like music: it must be composed by ear, feeling, and instinct, not by rule. But one had
better know the rules, for they sometimes guide in doubtful
cases, though not often." Vaughan Williams had undoubtedly
learnt the rules, with long and hard schooling. Whether or
not the rules he learnt were the right rules, they would not
contain the music he wanted to produce from within himself.
He was shyly observant of them, and assertively proceeded
to write down the sounds that were in his mind. The
struggle continued. He learnt his violin solo more surely by
practice in writing for voices with orchestra than by orchestral experiments.

At first the orchestra was for Vaughan Williams an
intractable medium; words, on the other hand, did not
baffle him. All the early time Vaughan Williams sought
English musical truth through English poetry. There was

little 'art-music' to guide him. But he climbed that stair.
As Dr Colles wrote:

> Many English composers have been happy in their choice of texts,
> because their language, wherever and however spoken, affords them
> peculiarly rich opportunities for their vocal music. Sometimes they
> have abused their privileges, so at least the poets from Milton
> onward have declared. Vaughan Williams's texts have always been
> chosen for some inner affinity between the poet's thought and his
> own. But he has never been dependent on a poetic text. A long
> series of purely instrumental works which ranges from the visionary
> *Fantasia on a Theme by Tallis* to a new symphony which few have
> heard and many await attests his freedom. All, vocal and instru-
> mental, large and small, display a character at once homely and
> remote; some would say mystical, for mysticism implies both. It
> is a character which only becomes fully articulate in musical notes.[1]

The work of Thomas Hardy provides an evident parallel.
When Hardy, the experienced prose-writer, turned to verse,
he found it equally intractable. Charles Williams has said
of the title of the first of the *Collected Poems*," The Temporary
the All,"

> At first there does appear something a little grotesque about it; it
> has an air of having been bullied into place. Hardy [Williams goes
> on, about words] has no pity for the tender things, and yet—
> apparently in love with so strict a master—they are glad to serve
> him, they delight to be employed even against their nature, and they
> will make for him the loveliest little songs directly after he has been
> compelling them to some intellectual hod-carrying.[2]

Just as Hardy "has not only changed prose into poetry; he
has, more surprisingly, changed poetry of one kind into
poetry of another," so, too, Vaughan Williams hammers
musical poetry out of a musical prose. He takes a conventional musical technique and makes an entirely novel music
out of it. These beginning pieces are struck out with rough
tools from a genuine but not finely polished metal plate;
they show that the composer had persistence, determination,

[1] *Op. cit.*
[2] *Poetry at Present* (Clarendon Press, 1930).

vision—almost every good quality but assured and fluent skill of hand. Despite his somewhat heavy-fisted technique, he certainly performed some amazing feats. If he could not manage the music with dexterity, he could manage the meaning of it and could 'bully' the notes to conform to his pattern. It is the job of every composer to learn to make an easy, flowing texture of his music. Some learn it early and readily, some later. Vaughan Williams learnt it later, and very thoroughly: but he always had meaning.

In the Fen Country was first played under Sir Thomas Beecham in 1907. The writer cannot recall incidence with the occasion. The score, seen to-day (in manuscript still), bears four dates in autograph: "composed April 1904, revised 1905 and 1907, orchestration revised 1935." As in a court of law, we must accept the evidence we are given. Nothing we can do now will bring back to us those first sounds, the spirits of those players. Memory cannot re-create the stirrings in the flow of the stream which, dispersed, have become a contributory part of the great river.

This "Symphonic Impression" gives us a picture of the countryside where Vaughan Williams found folk-song. Those frigid, misty mornings that make the journey from Cambridge to Ely so soul-searching a trek are portrayed here. Gloucestershire and the Severn are forgotten; not even the Trent is remembered. In this flat and watery part of England the sea is always near, the water seeps into the land, the tang of Holland stings the nostrils. No folk-songs are used as material for the composer's invention. It is a solid, well-drawn sketch, musical through and through—perhaps one might add that if one might dare to overlook the promise it displays, it is a little elaborate for the effect produced.

Of the *Three Norfolk Rhapsodies* only one[1] is known to me.

---

[1] The published version must differ from the original score. For this work seems to have made occasion for the first performance of Vaughan Williams's music outside England. On December 5, 1906, Walter Meyrowitz (for many years a well-known conductor in England with the Carl Rosa and other opera companies) played the First Norfolk Rhapsody at the Mozartsaal, in the Nollendorfstrasse, in Berlin. His programme notes quote five folk-songs ("*die man in der Grafschaft Norfolk in England singt*"); but in our score to-day only three remain.

They are the direct result of a spell of folk-song-collecting in January 1905 in the King's Lynn neighbourhood—a scene again strangely contrasted with his native West Country. The title-page of the "First Norfolk Rhapsody" states that it is "founded on folk-tunes collected orally in Norfolk and set as an orchestral piece." The adagio opening is as tenuous as a misty dawn, and there is a suggestion of the chilly vapours fluttered by a breeze from the sea. The viola sings to to us "The Captain's Apprentice"—one of the noblest and possibly the most directly tragic of English folk-songs; both words and music have a quality seldom to be found outside *Othello* and the Scottish ballads. "A bold young sailor courted me" rather shyly intrudes, and then "On board on a '98" takes over. The ending section never rises above *piano*, and closes in the sea mist of the beginning.

Though in a sense the "First Norfolk Rhapsody" might be called landscape painting, it is far more than a "symphonic impression"; it is a deeply considered work. If the grand orchestral clothes sit a little 'beginnerly' on the simple tunes, those tunes are allowed to walk their own way freely. The sum total is a moving piece of music which inspires and retains affection as well as admiration.

Apart from an excursus into incidental music for a Ben Jonson production at Stratford-on-Avon in 1905, the score of which is not extant, Vaughan Williams made his first contact with the theatre in 1909, when he was invited to write the music for the Cambridge production of *The Wasps* by Aristophanes. From the original score, which was designed for male-voice singers and orchestra, the composer made an orchestral suite of which the overture has attained a considerable popularity as a concert piece during the last few years. Tradition grew up during the late nineteenth century at both the major universities for undergraduate productions of Greek plays, with music specially composed for each occasion. Between 1880 and 1914 such music was provided by Macfarren, Parratt, Parry, Stanford, Charles Wood, and

Charles Harford Lloyd among others, and later, after the War, by younger composers like Dennis Arundell, Walter Leigh, and Patrick Hadley. For the previous production of *The Wasps* in 1897 the composer was T. Tertius Noble. These university productions are, as is proper in educational institutions, more concerned with the ebullient efforts of the actors than with the true meaning of the original authors or the theatre they wrote for. It would be as wrong to look for sublime tragedy on the Æschylean scale in Parry's *Agamemnon* or Stanford's *Œdipus Tyrannus* as to expect Aristophanic wit from the up-growing Vaughan Williams. The humour of his *Wasps* overture is not Attic, hardly even Doric. It is the slang talk of the undergraduate of the day, with a whole-tone melisma that is bordering on a pun. The wasps may buzz, but they are rather heavy-footed. An engaging, amateurish piece, full of jolly sounds and entertainment, with good tunes, firm and complete, it does not seem to rise from the ground, and one seems to hear the clumping steps of the adolescent actors. As a theatre-piece *The Wasps* overture is successful, for it is a good prelude to other music, and is designed to be listened to with only one ear. I have no doubt that the remainder of the music gave pleasure to many who knew little of Rogers and less of Calverley.

Theatrically *The Wasps* provides a bridge leading from early to later experience. The chance to write for the stage focused in Vaughan Williams's brain desires and designs that had been a-simmering in his soul since the interrupted meal at Munich, since Herzogenberg noticed the scent of Mascagni. Other factors (as the *Grove* article points out) came in—for example, a musical interest in the lives of the people. He was at this period in close consultation with Harold Child (of *The Times*) about an opera libretto which should bring a boxing-match on to the Covent Garden stage.[1] Not facile, Vaughan Williams's mind was enormously active. From about 1910–11 to 1914 *Hugh the Drover* was

[1] It never yet has.

H

under continued consideration—an odd by-play for a directed musical intention, but much needed, for it gave a wider outlet to an inherent musical bubbling which found itself inhibited by the sober conventions of the past and the continental exorbitancies meant to lead music to a new future. Vaughan Williams stayed where he was, and composed. As *Hugh the Drover* was not completed before the First World War and not produced until after 1918, I have kept consideration of it for the chapter on the stage works (pp. 175–187).

Despite the external references, the early music of Vaughan Williams is self-contained and satisfying in its own æsthetic design. The tonic-and-dominant cadence is avoided in new and various ways; as a pentatonist he has a liking for the subdominant. The rhythmic originality is more remarkable even than the harmonic. His freedom of rhythm, inspired by speech, as well as by other out-of-the-concert-hall methods of making continuous sound, breathed into the texture of the music a life not to be attained by mere technical readiness. Where this new English language stumbles we need do no more than remember our own daily fumbling attempts to manage the mere words of our tongue, so as to sympathize with him. Vaughan Williams is a man like ourselves, 'writ large.'

With a pictorial name, *The Lark Ascending* has a new quality of absoluteness in the musical pattern. Save in the opening and closing cadenzas—themselves interesting musically as well as imitatively—there would seem to be no literary or visual or associative source of inspiration except the composer's meditative mood. The title is taken from George Meredith's verses of the same name in his *Poems and Lyrics of the Joy of Earth*; prefaced to the score are some lines from the opening, middle, and closing of the poem.

> He rises and begins to round,
> He drops the silver chain of sound.
> Of many links without a break,
> In chirrup, whistle, slur and shake.

For singing till his heaven fills,
'Tis love of earth that he instils,
And ever winging up and up,
Our valley in his golden cup,
And he with wine which overflows
To lift us with him as he goes.

Till lost on his aërial rings
In light, and then the fancy sings.

This "Romance for violin and orchestra," as it is sub-titled, was written for and dedicated to Marie Hall—until her too early retirement in the nineteen-twenties one of the finest woman violinists in Europe. Finished in 1914, it had to wait till 1921 for performance and 1925 for publication. The orchestra required is small—two flutes, one oboe, two clarinets, two bassoons, two horns, triangle, and strings. Another version can be played by single wood-wind, one horn, and eleven or twelve strings. It has been a frequent practice with Vaughan Williams to make his orchestral works available for smaller combinations than those the music was conceived for—a practice which, though Sir Henry Wood (in *About Conducting*) arraigns it, was necessary until comparatively recently (and still is to some extent) if an English composer wanted his orchestral works performed. The *London Symphony*, for example, demands triple wood-wind, with two cornets and two harps, as well as the usual brass, percussion, and strings: but a note at p. 2 of the score tells us that the third flute, bass clarinet, and double bassoon parts can be omitted, the oboe merged with the cor anglais, and the cornets and trumpets condensed. On the whole it is better for the composer to 'cue in' instruments than to leave the job to the quick judgement of the conductor at a rehearsal or to mere chance omissions. Proper musical conditions should not necessitate it.

The lark ascends in a long melismatic cadenza. The quality of mind which makes this easy-looking string of unaccompanied intervals so individual and characteristic is not within description. Some part of it is no doubt the repeated third hanging from below the dominant, eventually becoming the opening of the main melody, and the centre-piece of a haunting phrase. Both this first melody and the second are coloured by the English folk-song, though neither has even a remote resemblance to any one recorded tune. The whole piece is as full of the sounds and scents of the English countryside as Keats's line "the murmurous haunt of flies on summer eves": it reminds one of John Clare, and Edward Thomas, and Edmund Blunden. Yet in the central music there is not a descriptive detail. One fortissimo (on strings alone, and repeated), two or three brief moments of forte, and nothing but quiet elsewhere. Wherein resides the exquisite charm of this work? It is certainly music of a new high level of beauty. The flow is easier, the development more subtle and concentrated, the song at once more restrained and more expressive, sheer beauty of sound more delicately achieved, than in the previous pieces. An original musical style is showing its first firm growth here, which will later flower into that magnificent creation, the *Pastoral Symphony*.

I have kept till last, out of its date order, the *Fantasia on a Theme by Thomas Tallis*, for double stringed orchestra and string quartet, because it occupies a separate place among the works of the earlier period. It was first performed under Sir Thomas Beecham at the Queen's Hall in 1909, and at the Gloucester Three Choirs' Festival in 1910. It is contemporaneous, therefore, with the *Sea Symphony*, earlier than the two cycles of mystical songs, but probably later than *On Wenlock Edge*. The string scoring is carefully balanced, and exacting in the disposition of the players in the concert hall: a note to the conductor printed at the head of the score reads thus:

The Second Orchestra consists of 2 First Violin players, 2 Second Violin players, 2 Viola players, 2 'Cello players, and 1 C'Bass player. These should be taken from the 3rd desk of each group (or in the case of the C'Bass by the 1st player of the 2nd desk), and should, if possible, be placed apart from the First Orchestra. If this is not practicable, they should play sitting in their normal places. The Solo parts are to be played by the leader in each group.

Four bodies of contrasting tonal strength, apart from the rhapsodic solo-passages, are by this method ranged in strategic line. The theme itself, written by that early composer of whose birth no record is known but who died in 1585 ("very aged," he is reputed to have said), appears in a modified form as No. 92 in *The English Hymnal*, and is a third-mode melody in a varying pulse of 3/4 and 6/8.

How long this complete work of art took in the making is not known. Internal evidence would suggest a long period, for the piece is a loving consideration of a single ancient tune; such commentary is hardly to be written in a journalist's spare moments. Within its self-set range it is completely satisfying. A single John drawing, a woman's face or limb roughed out by Michelangelo, an etching of a hare by Dürer—such small containers of genius have a lasting power over our minds, and it is the same power that the *Tallis Fantasia* wields. There is reason, as well, to believe that the piece is a first issue of the marriage of minds between Bunyan and Vaughan Williams which early began and lasts in his fine old age. Thoughts about the Pilgrim and his progress, as a subject for an opera, probably engendered this unique music.

So accustomed are we to the riot of colour in the Renaissance period in England, its blossoming in verse and music to a garden-full of flowers on every hand, that we are inclined to forget the inherent sense of tragedy, of philosophic solemnity, that was the loam below, nourishing all the golden splendour. Said Lear on the heath: "I am cold myself. Where is this straw, my fellow? The art of our necessities is strange, that can make vile things precious. Come, your hovel." Nashe wrote, some twelve or thirteen years earlier, in his "pleasant comedy," *Summer's Last Will and Testament*:

> Beauty is but a flower
> Which wrinkles will devour;
> Brightness falls from the air;
> Queens have died young and fair;
> Dust hath closed Helen's eye;
> I am sick, I must die—
>   Lord, have mercy on us!

In Dowland's short pieces can be found a melancholy unattained by the elaborations of the third act of *Tristan und Isolde*. The vein of sadness stretched its finger through the strata to touch the surface again in Purcell, that lively master-of-all-work in daily music, smiling his way through the difficulties of the 'new music' in Church, court, and theatre with equal ease, and yet in his personal vein writing music as vigorously sad as the direst scenes in Shakespeare or Æschylus. Never until this Fantasia by Vaughan Williams had that lode been mined again by an English composer.

Only a musical imagination of great power could at the same period plan and execute two musical methods of expression so oddly different as *A Sea Symphony* and the *Tallis Fantasia*. Against the energetic gales of the former the latter sets solid ramparts of concentrated thought. There is the stability of shelter, though not the resignation of the cloister. Shipwright's carpentry has given way to masonry. The English Cathedral is with us in the freshness of its birth, not in revived Gothic or steel girders clothed with machine-tooled ashlar; the blocks are in truth as rough and heavy as those that pattern the massive pillars of Durham Cathedral. The very Englishness of the *Fantasia* has, queerly, appealed to the foreigner: visiting conductors include the work in their programmes while they pass by pieces of more general attraction. For the *Fantasia* does not need either to attract or to startle. It stands four-square and if its sublimity does not exhilarate you, as a listener you will have to go away unsatisfied, uncompelled. But it compels.

For me the long struggles of English history, of men and Church and State, are chronicled in music in this score of nineteen folio pages. They hold the faith of England, in its soil and its tradition, firmly believed yet expressed in no articled details. There is quiet ecstasy, and then alongside of it comes a kind of blind persistence, a faithful pilgrimage towards the unseen light. Interested in orchestral effects as he was then growing to be, Vaughan Williams had shown greatest skill so far with the stringed instruments, as well as a sympathy for their colouring (especially in their lower hues). His practical work on hymnology helped his native Englishry towards love for the ancient tune. Its flowing and varied rhythm caught a mind already soaked by the sung rhythms of the English people; to these singing survivors the third mode was a natural language, akin to the plainsong of the Church. There is movement as well as deep thought, and the simple cadential figures were of the same kind as those of Vaughan Williams's own invention. The harmonic scheme need be no more than primitive: if it should wish to explore new country it has only to use the broad stepping-stones of common chords. These and no doubt many other circumstances fell together in time and place, and helped the sudden achievement of a completely original and personal style, without a hint of mannerism, while a springing invention served to blow the breath of life into the musical anatomy. The result was this incalculable and unexpected early masterpiece, the *Tallis Fantasia*.

The end of the vigorous first period was marked by the performance at Queen's Hall in 1914, under the late Geoffrey Toye, of the *London Symphony*—in dimensions the largest piece Vaughan Williams had so far conceived. It won him followers who had but faintly admired him before: growing out of a soil well-tilled by hard labour and varied sowings, it flourished, and became a landmark like the Ring on Chanctonbury Down or the Whittingham clumps around Wallingford or the white horses and the Cerne giant.

The English mind was unfolding itself in music, in accents not distinguishable from the voices of the English poets, but almost unrecognizable by the English people. To the musician these early "intimations of immortality" are important because no other composer since Byrd and his company, Purcell lagging behind, had justly translated our spoken and written language into an equally imperative musical speech. The Edwardian peace could not last, and the *London Symphony* leads us forward. Full understanding of Vaughan Williams's mind will, I think, best come from an intimate, musical study of these early works.

8

The Symphonies and Piano Concerto

VAUGHAN WILLIAMS has not himself numbered his symphonies. To the first three he gave specific labels, the other three he described merely by key: doubt, even then, seems to have been in his mind over the Fifth Symphony, for the original manuscript bore some notes at the opening and before the *Romanza* which do not survive in the printed score, and the delineation of key was at first G major (that of the opening movement) and then changed to D major (that of the finale).

It is tempting, and perhaps necessary, to regard these six works as a solid and complete historical monument, steady to the view. We are on safer ground than we were in 1940, when the fourth of the series, in F minor, had reached its fifth year of life. All *a priori* judgements were shattered by the appearance in 1943 of a fifth, of markedly different character. Those who settled down comfortably in the critical armchair with their revised judgement on their laps were again shaken out of complacency, five years later, by yet a sixth symphonic utterance, which, one cannot but feel, is a kind of summary and final development of all its predecessors. But, though the composer was nearing seventy-six when he wrote this last work, he would be an intrepid critic indeed who dared to assume that all the material for his final, considered estimate was before him. Stranger things have happened than that Vaughan Williams should add a seventh symphony to his list of compositions.

The Symphonies (and I include the Piano Concerto) do not appear to form a composite whole, like a single cathedral. They are rather a group of separate buildings, each put up at a different time to serve a different human purpose: a community of buildings, some for living and working in, some devoted to contemplation, some to the more decorative purpose of external beauty. Or one might make the comparison of an immense landscape: in symphonic terms Vaughan Williams lays out before our feet a vast and widely spreading tract of country, filled with man-made towns and fences, with natural and cultivated growths, with bare hills opening in a gap to show us the sea and the ships thereon, and to admit unobstructed the sea-winds.

The range of variety is remarkable, more so even than that in Beethoven's nine. The period Vaughan Williams's first six Symphonies span is thirty-eight years. Twenty-five years separate the *Sea Symphony* from the F minor, and already the differences are startling: the next thirteen years show no less change. This is, indeed, no static symphonic style, no mere roll of wallpaper from which the composer may cut lengths of the right dimensions to make a new work as like the last as possible. A less Straussian attitude towards music is not to be found. The language, though indubitably English, varies as much as the Englishes written by Shake-speare and T. S. Eliot. No composer is without his tricks of speech, but they are not noticeable here: could two large-scale melodies differ more than that in the *Sea Symphony*, mentioned at p. 94, from the second subject of the F minor's first movement? The former work has been criticized for the Wagnerean influence it shows: but the scale of the latter is infinitely more Wagnerean than the former. And neither of these works approaches in scale the philosophical mountain ranges that are the D major and E minor.

The symphonic procession may be described as a series of unexpected events, of unconventional utterances, punctu-ating the opening sentences of the twentieth century. Without entering upon the fascinating study of the relations between great events of history and major musical composi-tions following upon them, one may momentarily scan the dates of Vaughan Williams's Symphonies in their reference to certain international incidents of his period. The first two were written before the First World War, the second being revised during and after it; the next two come from the lull nicknamed "the long week-end," the other two respectively from the Second World War and the ensuing so-called peace.[1]

Music is the least topical of the arts: it is influenced by literary movements, by changes in civilization, more than by events, and wars, it would seem, apart from the usual journalistic spate of martial airs, tend to foster works of lasting merit expressing ideas unconnected with the shattering horrors or the victorious triumphs. Out of the 1914–18 conflict England produced only two major works on war subjects—Elgar's laureate-like *Spirit of England* and Arthur Bliss's *Morning Heroes*, the latter being a narrative of "battles long ago" and not of recent fighting. On the other hand, Gustav Holst was writing *The Planets* and *The Hymn of Jesus* in the 1915 period: in the trenches in Flanders Ivor Gurney sang "Do not forget me quite, O Severn Meadows": and Vaughan Williams's first large work after the war was the meditative *Pastoral Symphony*. The tortuous F minor relates in 1932–34 to no single incident, rather to a world-state of turmoil, and the second war-period resulted in the mystical and philosophical tranquillity of the D major. *Thanksgiving for Victory* was written after the War for a commission. Otherwise, only the "*Six Choral Songs*, to be sung in time of war" bears any relation to current events, and they, large-minded settings of Shelley, are neither topical nor of symphonic dimensions.

"The classic artist," wrote Havelock Ellis, "lives in a temple: the Romantic artist dwells in the forest." Vaughan Williams is not withdrawn: he lives among the living things, with men and trees and birds and (in mind if not in body) the sea for his daily companions. The first three Symphonies are concerned with actualities—the salt water, the city, the

[1] See "A Brief Chronology of Vaughan Williams's Main Extant Compositions" at pp. 202–203 of the present book to observe the incidence of the Symphonies among other works.

countryside. Excitement was caused in 1910 by the vivid optimistic freshness of the *Sea Symphony*, in 1914 and 1918 by the harsh picturesqueness of the *London Symphony*. ("London City," as Parry called it. His diary records: "March 27—To the Queen's Hall to hear Vaughan Williams's *London City*—full of interest and thought with fine effects of scoring.") Next, what Tovey has described as its "massive quietness" fell upon deaf ears in 1922, when the *Pastoral* was played. A quite different excitement was roused by the violent discords of the F minor in 1935, which made the strange noises of the *Mittel-Europa* atonalists look pallid by comparison. Remote though it may at first appear, this is really the Romantic symphony of the five: the forest has the terror by night rather than the arrow that flieth by day. The complex Romanticism is that of the late nineteenth century and earlier twentieth: the Romanticism of introspection. The D major (1943) won an easy hearing and a profound love and admiration by its persuasive philosophy. There is evidence of struggle, but the predominant feeling is the victory of spirit over matter: the wise thinker convinces us by his slow, kindly, contemplative talk. Only in the Sixth does Vaughan Williams approach "the temple," in Ellis's sense, and even then the pillars of his temple form aisles made rather out of tree-trunks than out of masonry.

These six works, together with the Piano Concerto—so bare in its thought, so uncompromising in its expression—tell the story of a mind schooling its thoughts into dramatic shape. The symphony is first and foremost a dramatic form, and there can be no doubt that Vaughan Williams was helped to the attainment of his symphonic mastery by his experience in operatic music. He learnt thereby to write narrative music, with its quiet moments of preparation, its touches of humour, as well as its compelling flow. From Brahms onward the symphony has taken to itself a solemnity that is positively portentous; it seems to wish to be a string of essential prophecies, an unending succession of memorable pronouncements of wisdom.[1] Precisely here the opera helped Vaughan Williams to make his symphonies living and flowing works, for he took us away from these 'high moral grounds' and led us to the truth.

The search for the exact expression of his meaning has always been Vaughan Williams's clearest aim and most troublesome difficulty. The medium would not always respond. "It is in the self-consciousness engendered by interference with spontaneity, and in aiming at a compromise to square with circumstances, that the real secret lies of the charlatanry pervading so much of English fiction," wrote Thomas Hardy in 1890. With the highest ideals of the symphony, and with an even rarer sense of size, Vaughan Williams has never tried to square his music into symphonic circumstances. His symphonies have made each its own circumstances: each is the outcome of a particular search for a particular truth.

The method of writing is not empirical. There is an absence of trial and error, as strongly felt as the absence of any wish to please. The symphony under Vaughan Williams takes on a new absolutism. He has his own inevitability. To say that the form is dictated by the material is too easy. Rather the material grows into a new semblance of a symphonic form, a semblance in the end exactly suited to its expression. But growing is a process accompanied by pains.

There are no purple patches, no sweet moments, in Vaughan Williams's symphonies. The broad, simple melody when it comes crystallizes within itself the turbulent meaning of what has gone before, of what may come after. A tune in the slow movement of the F minor Symphony, the simple song in the slow movement of the Piano Concerto, are summaries of thought—quiet climaxes, not quiet relief. "A sonata-movement may be said to be sewn together, a fugue to be woven," wrote Vaughan Williams in the article "Fugue" in Grove's *Dictionary of Music and Musicians*.

[1] But consult Tovey, *passim*, on "dominant preparation."

These symphonies, and particularly the Piano Concerto, are woven together; their constructive thought is continuous, but it is continuous in a dramatic way. Their drama is one of epic contemplation, not of visible incident; huge, full-scale, cosmic.

The scale is indeed remarkable; it is not even always achieved. The *London Symphony*, for example, falls short, for its idea is of a greater size than the achievement of the idea in the music. The oddity is that the magnitude of the idea even comes through the music, where it is, in my opinion, insufficiently realized. The *London Symphony*, as an experiment in symphony, leads to a direct denial of its own self in the ensuing works in the same form. The long discussions are spontaneously but not tautly argued. Yet the effort of the thought led to a fine logical reasoning in the later works. The Piano Concerto, on the other hand, makes no similar error: in it the composer has managed his uncomfortable medium (for, as we know, he has no natural feeling for the keyboard) in exact proportion between thought and musical expression. He has here, by hard mental process, completely welded form and matter.

As for the weaving method itself—that is, the texture of fugue—both the F minor and the Piano Concerto use fugue in their last movements as a means of completing a dramatic design by a logical argument. The *Pastoral Symphony* is contrapuntal in the warp and woof of its texture, though symphonic in design and dramatic in the very persistence of its thoughtful mood. The finale of the D major is a *passa-caglia*, and the scherzo of the E minor was described by the composer in his own programme note as "fugal in texture but not in structure."

Shakespeare is ever present in these symphonies; they are in the Shakespeare line. Closer in technical method of construction (but not in modes of thought) is the affinity with Thomas Hardy, for some of us also in the Shakespeare line. Edmund Blunden's book on Thomas Hardy in the "English Men of Letters" series aptly demonstrates, if it did not originate thought of, the resemblance. From both that book and its reviews whole sentences about Hardy can be culled which, with minor technical alteration of terms, apply to Vaughan Williams. I quote one review only, from *The Times Literary Supplement* of February 21, 1942:

> There is no author of comparable knowledge and reflection of whose work it is so tempting to say that "it comes like that." He was feeling his way: he followed his course faithfully. Sometimes the thing he was after turned out to be what he had hoped for, or very nearly as good. Sometimes it did not: and he was left with a result which may have surprised him, most probably disappointed him, but was nevertheless (subject to revision by a little still more careful fingering) what the thing had turned out to be. One can hear him say, "So that is what it was!" in all tones of delight or dissatisfaction.

Many aspects of comparison may be seen: the absence of dogmatism, for example, the expression of discovered personal truths as 'seemings.' Vaughan Williams has a sense of open spaces: like Hardy in his novels, he can create distances in his music. But his landscapes are not described or pictured to us. Holst, in *Egdon Heath* (so consciously 'Hardy'), attempts to give us an impression of that countryside between Bere Regis and Wimborne which most deeply influenced Hardy's youth. But Vaughan Williams's London and country live only in his music, not in their associations. There is no 'pathetic fallacy.' They are principal characters in the drama, just as the "cliff without a name," the woodlands round Melbury Osmond, the stone pits of Portland, and the "dreaming spires" are principal characters in Hardy's novels.

Moreover, in Vaughan Williams, as in Hardy, the human element recedes as the style grows in accomplishment. The *London Symphony* is as full of local colour as *The Mayor of Casterbridge*, almost as full as *Under the Greenwood Tree* (which is, in nearer comparison, to be matched with *The Lark Ascending* and the *Five English Folk-songs*). In the *Pastoral Symphony* we stand farther back: *The Return of the*

Native uses the landscape more impersonally as part of the
tragedy of Clym Yeobright and Eustacia Vye, of dear
Thomasin and her mother and Damon Wildeve, the expression in whose eyes (far more than Eustacia's) is dark with the
colour of the November furze. The F minor Symphony is as
epic as *The Dynasts* in its remote yet understanding contemplation of human strife: while in the Fifth and Sixth of the
series there is reached a height of contemplation never
attained completely by Hardy in his fiction, but sought and
found by Hardy the poet on his sixty years' journey of
verse-writing.

By this time we have left the idea of 'subject-painting' in
a dusty corner, a discarded ladder (as it were). We are near
to that method of reproduction of an object in its entirety
and many-sidedness which Matthew Arnold has called
"imaginative reason." Sibelius had it, in a degree, by
nature; Vaughan Williams fought to find it. His Symphonies show the incidents of that fight, round by round,
battle by battle. Arthur MacDowall described Hardy, in a
phrase, as "a historian of life." So, in another, less defining
medium, is Vaughan Williams. But, once more, dates can
give us a new angle of illumination. Hardy was born in
1840, Vaughan Williams in 1872. The second date is that
of *Far from the Madding Crowd*. Hardy was a Victorian
rebel; he ceased writing novels in 1896, because *Jude the
Obscure* ("obscene") met with so cold a damnation. Vaughan
Williams did not properly begin till years later. As in most
movements of civilization, with the *Nuove Musiche* no less
than with Goethe and Thomas Gray, music expressed some
forty and more years later what literature had foreseen, and
to some extent could crystallize the tendencies of the thought
of the time. "Poets," not composers, "are the trumpets that
sound to battle, poets are the unacknowledged legislators of
the world." Yet, the composers, telling a larger world in
more easily accepted terms the kind of things the poets have
said, become, after the proper interval, the prophets of the
new thought. Beethoven reaches to-day tens of thousands of

hearts for whom Goethe is a name unpronounceable, a writer unreadable in an alien tongue. Maybe Vaughan Williams is doing unconsciously a similar thing for our own 'modern' period.

A Sea Symphony[1] is the unquestioned title which the composer gave to the choral piece that bears it. Consideration of the work as a turning-point in the composer's career and in his mental development has occupied earlier attention, at pp. 90–98 of this book. It is necessary, however, to assess it in symphonic relation to its five successors. Judgement of the work as a symphony, however, is no easy matter, for it hardly fits into the pattern. Whether hearers would have thought of it as a symphony at all, despite its four movements, had not the composer's intention been so clearly indicated, may be doubted, though one can imagine oneself writing in some such terms as "this choral work of symphonic design and shape." For that is what it is. No Godmade rule governs symphonic form: good definitions abound, all at variance. Cecil Gray is particularly illuminating on the subject in his *Sibelius*[2]: Tovey in another way: the text-books differ widely, from both and from each other.

Neither academics nor critics have sole right of tenure. One observes a progressive humanization of the symphony absolute from the *Choral Fantasia* and Ninth all through the rest of the century. Berlioz in *Romeo*, Liszt in the *Faust* and *Dante* Symphonies, Mahler in his Third, Fourth, and Eighth, bring voices into the orchestral pattern. No one, however, before 1910, had put forward the voices and the words they sing as determining the whole symphonic development, the entire formal shape of the continuation of the music: few have since (save Holst and Bantock, for example). The voices have the music, the orchestra is no

---

[1] Detailed analyses of most of the Symphonies and the Piano Concerto can be found in the three volumes of "The Musical Pilgrim Series" (Oxford University Press), one by A. E. F. Dickinson, the other two by Frank Howes; and Tovey has treated the *Pastoral* in *Essays in Musical Analysis*, vol. ii (Oxford University Press, 1935).

[2] Pp. 127–131 (Oxford University Press, 1934).

more than elaborate accompaniment, a helper of texture rather than of continuity of thought.

The 'programme' appears to be self-confessed. Actually it is not. The 'programme' seems to consist of Whitman's ideas, and they lead the music. But the moods of the music are induced by considerations other than the words, by the ideas of the sea which the American poet (a Long Islander) conjures up in the mind of the English musician (a Gloucestershire man). The moods are Vaughan Williams's. First, in the music, comes his expression of his own ideas— in the opening movement, the universal brotherhood of shipmates in a fluid danger; secondly, a silent thinker on the shore; thirdly, a boisterous incoming tide; the fourth movement is a rather complicated mixture of Whitman and Vaughan Williams, and, though the words are dramatically set, the mood-painting has less sway than the thought behind the words. Yet this is the best of the four movements on musical assessment.

Vaughan Williams, then, has jumped off the springboard of Whitman to make his own pictorial ideas of the sea and its silent service of ships, with men in them. Led by the words, he manages to make "a remarkable achievement in the embodiment of the moods in which it deals." Those words were written in Grove's *Dictionary* by the great American critic and scholar, Richard Aldrich (*quondam* of the *New York Times*) about the *London Symphony*. They apply here to my argument.

The *Sea Symphony*, seen in perspective, seems shadowy as a symphony. The dimensions, the scale of intentions, are right. The four conventional movements confront us. I feel, in the end, that this work is a series of pictures brilliantly put before us in an enticing gallery, four separate paintings of a great and mobile subject, yet not quite making the whole that a symphony must be. My love for the work does not diminish with the careful consideration of years. But I find its freshness of utterance, not its symphonic form, its greatest quality.

Salvador de Madariaga, in one of his penetrating occasional essays on national characteristics, attributes the Englishman's deficiency in sense of form to "his predominant interest in action." This "action-sense" he finds to contain "something of the puritan and perhaps even of the ascetic spirit." The Germans in their music he calls "mist-sculptors."

In *A Sea Symphony* can be found, for all its breezy vigour, something of the puritan and something of the ascetic, far less of the mist-sculptor. In *A London Symphony*, on the other hand, there is a predominance of the mist-sculptor over even the ascetic of its rising fourths and fifths; and the mist-sculptor applies himself to his task purposefully. True, the mist is the literal city, the English capital half visible under the fog, and the sculpture is the making of a new and original kind of English musical masonry.

It has been recorded that when Sir Henry Wood played the work in Rome in 1935 the audience was so enthusiastic as to demand a second performance of the entire work. That is but one example of a phenomenon observable throughout its public career—the extraordinary grip with which this Symphony fastens upon those who hear it for the first time. It has the power of making an immediate effect that is not only profound but lasting. For many who heard it at its performances in 1914 and 1918 the *London* remains the first great symphony in our native language, nor does it pale in the memory, stale in the later hearings. At least two generations of English musicians, and many hundreds of music-lovers, have accepted it as a permanent part of the English heritage.

A London Symphony is crowded with ideas and tunes and incidents. The cockneys are hit off to a 't' in the livelier parts: the spontaneous cheekiness of the airs, as well as their hammered-out construction, prevent them from becoming mere *pastiche*. The varied rhythms are fascinating, if sometimes they give the impression of being a little uncertain,

like a hiccough. There is now and then the peace of Wordsworth on Westminster Bridge:

> Never did sun more beautifully steep
> In his first splendour, valley, rock, or hill;
> Ne'er saw I, never felt a calm so deep;

and Big Ben (on the harp) chimes in opportunely. The
fragmentary phrases are subjected to a constructive process
of development that recalls (but could not be reminiscent of)
the Sibelius Symphonies. In the second movement there is
a beautiful moment of crystallization of silence—a fine idea
finely expressed. The scherzo (London at night, the title
suggests) has vibration, the movement of distant trams and
trains crossing the bridges over the river. There are
stationary moments of arabesque, as we stop in the street
and listen. The mouth-organ, and the jolly tune over it, are
good fun. The march in the last movement is impressive
and speaks of London's sombreness, of birth and death:
after the *con fuoco* we meet a logically planned moment of
repose. And so to the Epilogue that links first movement
with fourth, Big Ben again helping as usher.

Personal affection and considered admiration apart, I am
bound to confess that I do not think *A London Symphony*
wholly successful as a symphony. It is possible that what
leads me to this conclusion is exactly what makes it so
striking a work at a first hearing. The pictorial details aid
the listener, for they arrive aptly in the musical pattern. I
entertain no doubt about the largeness of the work; my
doubt is whether it is large enough, whether it is always
large. The scheme is almost grandiose; but I find that it
overwhelmed the composer, that he had difficulty in living
up to it, and that the picturesque details are called in for too
frequent assistance.

No matter if the composer started from noises heard in
the streets, and built his edifice with the discarded bricks
lying around on untenanted plots. The eventual plan still
seems to override the musical technique. Big in spite of

itself, *A London Symphony* does not appear to me to solve the symphonic equation. It has a fine swing, the forward rhythm of a vast ship or a huge tide. We move on, all the time, but some of the time we seem only to be poised in the wind, waiting for the next one of a series of incidents. The dramatic conflict occurs between musical ideas rather than with personified characters. Vaughan Williams, at this stage, clothed his musical ideas with external happenings; or, alternatively, in reverse, he took his ideas already clothed and tried to strip them down to their bare musical skeletons. My view is that he dramatized London in a symphony. Ears, eyes, and heart went into the process of London's decoction. In a country where opera is not a native growth but, so far, mainly a visitor, he crammed an opera into a symphonic mould. *A London Symphony* is too picturesque to be admissible as a pure symphony, but it is so living as to be lovable as a gigantic *scena*, cast into a form that need not use the visual stage, the colours and lights and costumes. What else could he do at that moment in English life with the vivid exteriorities of his imagination? The physical objects, the visions seen and heard and noticed, were whipped into submission to a symphonic scheme which, then, was the only acceptable medium (save the chorus) for an English composer who aimed at fulness of expression.

Nineteen-hundred-and-fourteen was a time of the breaking of nations; an old world met its death throes. The changing world is material for historians. Great changes were also taking place in the mind of Vaughan Williams; in the eight years that divide the first version of the *London* (1914) from the *Pastoral* (1922) he seems to have become musically a different man. The mental changes can only be discovered by a study of his music. It is not surprising that those who knew no more of his mind than the *London*, and perhaps *On Wenlock Edge*, should have found the *Pastoral* incomprehensible. But, it is suggested here, the proper approach to the latter work is along the path of his earlier music, which leads gently over the foothills towards this isolated peak.

The two symphonies are oddly contrasted. In the earlier the composer was addressing an audience, in the later he was talking to himself.[1] The one dramatized external things, attitudinized here and there, was objective, anthropo-morphic, theatrical, and splendid. On the contrary, the other was concerned with ideas, impersonal and ruminative, subjective, absolute, chamber-music-like, and pale (or 'of low values') in colouring. From *A London Symphony* one can quote, never from the *Pastoral*. Where the former is detailed the other is vague. And yet, the queerest contrast of all is that while at first glance the Symphony about London may seem to be the firmer and more solid in struc-ture, actually that about the countryside is the more archi-tectural in the conception of its design, the more carefully wrought in the construction, and at once the larger and the closer-knit in the execution of the symphonic pattern.

"Poetry," wrote James Stephens once,

> is a very private matter, and is only communion with others by their merit, and by their identity with solitary song. All poetry that is widely and immediately acceptable is a peasant poetry, and is almost a parody of everything that poetry intends and promises. For poetry intends your freedom, and promises you beauty.

Paradoxically, London as a subject drew the peasant out of Vaughan Williams; the country drew out of him the poet and philosopher. Dr Herbert Howells sums up the music thus: Vaughan Williams

> neither depicts nor describes. It is not his concern to "make the universe his box of keys." He builds up a great mood, insistent to an unusual degree, but having in itself far more variety than a merely slight acquaintance with it would suggest. Even its detractors (and they may be many) will admit its compelling sense of unity, though they count it death to the work. If you like, it is a frame of mind

[1] "There was an element of 'damn the consequences' about the first performance," wrote Dr Herbert Howells (*Music and Letters*, April 1922, vol. iii, No. 2). This essay, from which further passages are quoted here by permission of author and editor, is at once a penetrating exposition of the work and a valuable inquiry, by a practitioner, into the methods of composing the music of to-day.

(not consciously promoted). The country is that: so, too, is any place, village or town. You may not like the Symphony's frame of mind; but there it is, strong and courageous; it is the truth of the work, and out of it would naturally arise whatever risk it has run of being cold-shouldered.[1]

For myself, I have written of my 'affection' for the two predecessors. For the *Pastoral* I have reverential awe as well as deep love; the music gives me a key to the central thoughts of one of the great English minds of our time. Eschewing all local reference, the composer paints the English land-scape in music with the "light that never was on sea or land." There is no 'meaning' save in the music, which is logical and not impressionistic. To express his thoughts about the world of natural growths Vaughan Williams uses no symbols, calls up no memories by audible reference to known objects, paints us no picture of his or others' delight in the events of the season or the occurrences of climate. "The mood of this Symphony," wrote the composer in his first programme note, "is almost entirely quiet and contemplative." His frank words do not contain the vast, silent spaces of his thought, as he stands in mute contemplation. The human voice that heralds and closes the finale is a disembodiment, the spirit of man ecstasized as in a morality or in one of Blake's drawings. We are, in this work, brought at one with the universe, each of us able to "see the world in a grain of sand" which is a millionth part of our garden path.

The technical methods of the *Pastoral* are entirely new to symphony. The idiom itself, personal though it be, is not unfamiliar—that is to say, the words themselves are not strange, so much as the way they are grouped into sentences, paragraphs, and chapters. We find at the opening the rising fourth and fifth which also characterize the first movement of the *London*. The succession of contiguous common chords recurs, with even a semi-quaver run as before. Others of the fingerprints are visible. Yet nothing quite like it ever came before this music. The texture of the *Pastoral* is almost

[1] *Op. cit.*

entirely melodic and contrapuntal. "'Tune' never ceases," writes Dr Howells; he goes on:

> one after another come tributary themes, short in themselves, and so fashioned as to throw one into doubting their being new; one suspects that, in them, what was a part has become a whole.

But here are melody and counterpoint with a difference. The melody could not have grown from any seed but English folk-song, to which it bears, however, no immediate or traceable resemblance. On another page Dr Howells says:

> None of the tunes in the [*Pastoral*] Symphony have exciting lines. I recall that a distinguished composer once showed me the profile of Napoleon by drawing a line through the notes of the first subject of Beethoven's Third Symphony. One might get queer caricatures by similarly experimenting on Stravinsky's themes. Vaughan Williams's tunes will not 'draw faces,' or produce crude pictures of craggy heights. But they will often give you a shape akin to such an outline as the Malvern Hills present when viewed from afar.

And as for the counterpoint, it is characterized less by some broad contrary motion than by a persistence of similar motion. The curves tend to follow each other in parallel layers, with strange harmonic effects which Tovey has described by the coined word 'polymodality.' Melisma abounds, both in the form of figuration in accompaniment and in the veiling of subsidiary melodic phrases, and also in frequent recitative passages for solo instruments, which find their final development in the long solo passages for single soprano voice that envelop the last movement.

A large orchestra is demanded, three flutes, two oboes and cor anglais, three clarinets (one taking bass clarinet), two bassoons, four horns, three trumpets, three trombones, bass tuba, drums, two percussion players, harp, celesta, soprano voice, and strings. Yet there is hardly a moment of forte, never a sustained fortissimo in the whole work. In the hearing the ear meets two especial points—the curious and novel delicacy of the continuously peaceful sound, and the close resemblance this extensive band of players bears to a small chamber-music group. The Symphony loses nothing in size, is no less massive or weighty, for its eternal quietness and its refusal of violent dynamic contrasts. The movements do not act as foils to each other; different though they come to be as one discovers the work, they are somewhat similar in tonal pattern. The unceasing flow of unchecked rhythms, resembling the steady progress of a river towards the sea, do not prevent the *Pastoral* from having a static quality which reminds one, in a way, of *Pelléas et Mélisande*. Like that opera, it engenders its own, new dramatic power out of its contemplative stillness.

Wide as the gap is between the *London* and the *Pastoral* Symphonies, it is as nothing to the cleavage between the *Pastoral* and its successor in F minor—the fourth of the series and the first designated by key and not by a title. The whisperings of the former were audible to the intelligences of but few, whereas the latter's stridency shocked the hearing, and, indeed, the sensibilities, of nearly all who heard it. As an essay in discord to "split the ears of the groundlings," "it out-herods Herod." There is more than outspokenness here; there is a studied harshness, invented and used deliberately for the expression of the new symphonic idea. In spite of the initial surprise that it causes in most listeners, the F minor Symphony presents less difficulty in its method of construction than in its actual musical idiom. As a symphony it is straightforward in plan compared with the *Pastoral*. The growth of its elaborate pattern out of two main units is easy to follow at a first hearing; the acceptance of the discordant idiom may well prove to be a less readily surmountable barrier. Constructionally it not only approaches the absolute in musical thought more closely than any previous work by Vaughan Williams (even *Flos Campi*), but it is, in fact, the most purely logical of his compositions to that date.

There is not a shadow of a 'programme,' not a hint of extra-musical association, and yet I do not think it fanciful to relate this stupendous work—one that only reveals its full size after long study—to the state of the world in the early nineteen-thirties, when it was written (in sketches 1931, in completion and performance 1935). Delicacies are thrust aside. A new truth of violent force has been discovered, and a new language of equal violence has been invented to express its full meaning. The composer writes the notes he wants, not more but not less, without fear or a desire to please. The tragedy is Æschylean in scale, a kind of *Götterdämmerung*, only the gods are not disembodied figures but merely those human beings who are ourselves. The Symphony is perhaps more prophetic of tragedy in the future than descriptive of it in the past. We meet in it something of the horror and the almost agonizing beauty of John Webster. At times there come into the mind Gloucester's words to the old man on the heath in *King Lear*: "As flies to wanton boys, are we to the gods; They kill us for their sport." There enters at this moment a Lear humour—that of the King, not of Edward. The man-made gods are laughing at us, and not with us. The fall of the world is a gigantic joke, but it affects us, each one, with personal disaster.

The devil drives along the road in this Symphony—that is, perhaps, why in earlier words I called it the 'Romantic' Symphony. But, in our troubles, the composer gives us something of human pity. The work is worldly, but it is not definite in reference; it deals with all of us as one unit, but remembers that each of us is one unit within a larger unit. Cosmic in scale, it does not aspire to the universal. The Earth, not the Sun or Sirius, is its province.

The musical idiom is odd; so is that of the *Pastoral*. But the *Pastoral*'s idiom is full of English speech, full of things so English that no one dared to use them before in music, whereas the F minor adopted the semitone and seventh. There are no mannerisms. The new language does not struggle, it is inexorable, sweeping away aural barriers as it marches along. The rhythm helps, naturally, for the F minor has a sweep of the incoming tide, of a gale and a storm and a succession of towering waves, not to be observed in the avowed *Sea Symphony*. The slow movement gives little relief. An unheard sound reaches our ears—neither tonal nor modal, not even atonal—something visioned remotely by the writer and given to us in exact denomination of black dots upon the paper (so hard to read silently here!). It would, perhaps, not be accurate to call this Symphony 'experimental,' for the accomplishment is so carefully achieved. Sounds occurred in the composer's brain, and he fought, and won, the battle of putting them down in such commands as the players could obey. The orchestration is interesting; the brass instruments have parts to play which are not to be found in Wagner's scores: yet we know Vaughan Williams heard them. The absoluteness of this Symphony does not abide only in his first philosophic thoughts; it abides also in his instrumentation. Another point—this logical work, in four differing movements (though all are provocative), is linked into one whole by the use of a central motive, with other subsidiaries, and derives some of its later material from music which has been heard before, in other guise. This characteristic it is which made Mr Frank Howes use, in his analysis, the excellent phrase, "No wonder a structure braced in both directions is strong."[1] The overcoming factor, swamping originality of idiom and construction, is the Titanic rhythmic urge, the flood of the music as it throws us out of its way to make its channel clear.

Closely though they fit together as part of an integral conception, linked thematically, the four movements are well contrasted. Each hearer will find a different quality in them, perhaps a different one at each successive hearing. For me it is the large scale of the first movement that is impressive, rather than the harsh candour of its harmony. The 'second subject,' introduced unexpectedly soon over pulsations on the wind, is of vast size, and Vaughan Williams

[1] *The Later Works of Vaughan Williams* ("Musical Pilgrim Series," Oxford University Press, 1937).

keeps just proportion by the spaciousness of his treatment and the broad calm of the coda. The andante moderato is a carefully reasoned argument of somewhat bare premises, which in themselves are derived from propositions stated in the first movement. Treatment is at times contrapuntally close, but as the thematic material grows it develops more open phrases. The successions of syncopated falling fourths haunt the memory. The scherzo whirls us along at breath-taking speed, with a ruthless, caustic humour. Angular fragmentary themes coalesce into a broad statement, and lead to the strange caperings of the trio (a fugato on an allied theme). Without a break, but with exciting preparation, the finale bursts on us: here the floods seem to break all the dams, and pour over us in an overwhelming torrent. The humour takes on a cynical air of *braggadoccio*, with an aptly contrived "oompah bass" (so called in the composer's own programme notes). Despite quieter episodes, a thrusting energy carries us along into the *Epilogo Fugato*; where the discordant material from the first movement is displayed in a kind of foreshortening that seems almost out of drawing, like an exaggerated caricature, but is in fact a resolution of all the arguments the music has pursued in its relentless course. It need only be added, about this towering Symphony, that no music like it had ever been written before, by Vaughan Williams or anyone else, nor has any since.

Nearest in kinship to it is the Piano Concerto, which was played in London almost exactly two years before the Symphony (February 1, 1933). Indeed, these two works are, for me, inextricably bound together. There are differences, of course—that of size, for example—but there are also similarities. Something of the same humour is expressed, especially in the rackety finale; something too of the demoniac energy; a relentless driving-power thrusts both works along like a ship against a head-wind. But the Concerto moves more slowly, and with a heavier tread; the pace is more deliberate, with less of majesty, more of tenderness (the slow movement of the Concerto is touchingly human, while the F minor gives mankind but poor harbourage from "the storms of fate"). There are similarities of idiom too, including the unfamiliar discordance. But the language of the Concerto is terser, and even more literal, than that of the Symphony. The literal quality is particularly to be found in the writing for the pianoforte, which Vaughan Williams treats throughout as percussive, not only in its mechanism but in its proper method of expression. In the Concerto Vaughan Williams seems to have reached, following his own English by-ways, a place not far away nor very different in its landscape from that to which, in later life, Bartók led us along his Hungarian paths. Apart from the piano-writing, the language of the Concerto deviates less than that of the Symphony from that conglomerate language which, for convenience, we may call the composer's central mode of speech. There are familiar mannerisms: the long rising tune in the bass, the tonal melismas, the successive fourths and fifths in the first movement, and in the second the slow, simple, pregnant melodies; even in the discordant finale we recognize the tone of voice.

The inclusion of the Piano Concerto in this chapter on the Symphonies suggests in itself that I do not consider it a true Concerto. "If the wine is to our liking," wrote Hadow, "it is sheer ingratitude to pick holes in the label." I have no intention of doing so, counting the work as better fitted for a place in this chapter than in a later one on account of its symphonic qualities, which outshine its interest as an ensemble of soloist and orchestra. On its first appearance the work was found perplexing; it was not liked then, nor have either soloists or conductors (not even critics) taken to it since. Lack of personal success can be understood, and partially explained by other reasons than that it was different from the accepted, printed notions about piano concertos. (It is, in fact, near to being unique.) Some reasons may be hinted at—for example, an even more experimental technique in sound was used than in the F minor, for this new medium was strange and rough ground for the composer's feet. The keyboard was like a prickly hedge in his path. Then, it must be admitted, the Concerto does not 'come off' as the Fourth Symphony does; not every note is compelling of audition, and, as a result, individual points of idiom tend to become enlarged into wilful oddities.

The soloist's part is (as I have said) percussive; it is also powerful and massive. I have not yet heard one pianist play it as the notes are meant to sound. Muscles of steel, a ruthless dominance over the orchestra, no fear of stridency or of ugly hitting—in the pianist's offertory these are essentials for the player of the Concerto. He cannot easily force his sounds through the orchestra, and when (as often) he has the principal voice in the music's argument, then, especially when he is playing alone, he needs to rattle his concert-machine with a vigour both incisive and weighty.

Suggestions were made to the composer, after the first performance, by Adrian Boult and others, that better balance and registration could be attained if he were to re-score the work for two pianos and orchestra. After a lapse of years he complied with the proposal, and invited the pianist Joseph Cooper to make, as a collaborator, a new version which Phyllis Sellick and Cyril Smith first performed in 1946.[1] For myself, I prefer, and believe in, the original scoring for single piano with orchestra; only, a pianist of a special kind is needed to play it. Pianistically the soloist's part is not so much difficult as curious and unexpected in its demands. I remain convinced that it is successful in carrying out the intention that was in the composer's mind, and I both like and admire that intention.

The Piano Concerto is a complicated structure of fairly short phrases. But the fabric is not that of a mosaic; rather it is that of freestone in a heavy building. The three movements are joined. The second owes nothing thematically to the first, but seems to flow out of it; the finale builds the

[1] The work is available in both versions, but it should be noted that the reduction made by Miss Vally Lasker for two pianos for rehearsal purposes, one representing the orchestral part, refers only to the version for single piano.

pinnacle of the work, in the soloist's climax, out of stones first roughly hewn for use in the slow movement. No Malvern Hills' outlines mark these rugged phrases; they have a Euclidean angularity, without, however, being mathematical or inhuman. Aggressive to begin with, the first movement broadens out into a statement more positive and assertive, less dare-devil. In strange contrast is the ruminative mood of the slow movement; the beautiful opening melody is couched in a language so simple as to be almost baffling. The central episode—Vaughan Williams at his most transcendent—is important in the design of the work, for all its tenderness and beauty; out of it flowers the figure that is soon to become the subject of the *Fuga Chromatica*. A chromaticism strange in Vaughan Williams makes a riotously successful fugue. To this final movement the pianoforte contributes more than to the other two; it is almost a piano rhapsody with orchestral background, and yet there is nothing about it of the show-piece. The pianist holds the music. Thus in the cadenza there is a kind of summary of the entire work; but all we have heard is only preliminary to the finale *alla tedesca*, where the soloist may not "dance barefoot on her wedding day," but certainly "leads apes in hell," with a Mephistophelian sense of fun. The second cadenza makes the true climax of the work, which ends with a derisive gesture, in the most adult sense.

The chasm that divides the fifth of the symphonies from the fourth is equally precipitous to that which divides fourth from third. But it is, oddly, not the chasm of war. The terrestrial crater has been formed rather by the power of poetic vision than by mere high explosives. But, whatever the cause of the earthquake, it has thrown us up on to solid earth that has a familiar look, a landscape new perhaps but easily recognizable, rather as if we had had a fore-glimpse of it in a dream. Both in idiom and in symphonic method the D major is original and unexpected—I mean, that no one could have deduced them as the logical outcome of preceding musical processes in the composer's mind. Yet there are features of the view which, even on a first meeting, we remember—somewhat vaguely, perhaps, and tardily, with a touch of that shamefaced feeling we experience when we say, "I'm sure I've met that man before. Gracious me! He and I were at school together!" We have arrived (it is borne in upon us) at the place we were seeking—the end of our symphonic journey, that we always knew was ahead of us, but could not ourselves describe before we had actually seen it. Here, in fresh invention, is the complete fusion of all Vaughan Williams's symphonic essays—in form, in matter, in manner; we have come home at last, even if, through the passing of years, home has an appearance that it never quite had before.

It might appear, perhaps, that the problematical sixth of the series—in E minor—dispels this dream, and exorcises the ghosts of the past. With any such appearance or view I must express disagreement. Both in idiom and in symphonic method the E minor is an extension of the D major. The ideas expressed in them differ, of course; but they are alike in their musical procedures, and can therefore be classed together with less manifest improbability than any other two of the symphonies, align them how you will.

Public appreciation of the D major was more immediate than that of perhaps any other single work by the composer. The circumstances of time and place can be partly discounted —the fact of the composer's age, the availability of music through radio, the contrast of the music's peace with the noise of war. Of those circumstances perhaps the most interesting was the temper of unity among the English peoples which war had induced. "Britain," writes Mr Winston Churchill of June 1940, "was united as never before"; it may be speculative to think that "the general" found in 1943 a recognizable English voice of comfort and prophecy in this work. The feeling has not, I admit, lasted, for six years later "the general" have sunk back once more into the old neglect of their own composers. English musical speech hardly even irritates the complacent torpor.

The character of the Symphony itself was, I think, mainly responsible for its first wide appeal.

The D major Symphony is in every way different from the recent war in Europe. It is democratic, universal, in its attitude to mankind; it is slow, contemplative, kindly, and philosophical in outlook. There is never an attempt to dominate—to bowl you first ball, or to win five miles' territory of your thought by *Blitzkrieg*. The philosophy persuades, as the philosophy of a wise thinker of experience in life. We lack no evidence of struggle, but the victory is, in the main, that of soul over materialism. The thinker takes us by the hand and leads us—willing travellers—over the rougher places to a valley where we can contemplate, in a blessed silence, both the wisdom of the ages and the folly of brutality in war-sought ambition. We meet no pacifism nor Communism nor any other 'ism.' We meet only the wisdom of religion, of the Bible, of John Bunyan.

The original manuscript score, which I was privileged to study in 1943, bore certain verbal annotations which (I record with some regret) have not been allowed to survive in the printed pages. First, the Symphony was dedicated, originally, in these words: "without permission and with the sincerest flattery to Jean Sibelius, whose great example is worthy of imitation." Secondly, the opening page bore the note: "some of the themes of this Symphony are taken from an unfinished opera, *The Pilgrim's Progress*."[1] Thirdly, the slow movement, named *Romanza*, was prefaced by a motto, a quotation from Bunyan's *Pilgrim's Progress* itself: "Upon this place stood a cross, and a little below a sepulchre. Then he said: 'He hath given me rest by his sorrow, and life by his death.'" (At this moment Christian, the Pilgrim, was burdened heavily, and ran up a high way fenced on either side by the wall called Salvation. He was glad and lightsome, and spoke with a merry heart.)

These first-thought literary adjuncts to the staves and

[1] At the time of writing the opera has been completed and played, in first draft and piano reduction, to a company of friends.

K

note-heads seem to me to have value in illuminating the hidden places of the composer's mind at that phase of its creative growth. It may be permitted, therefore, to peer at the work from the gazebo that they provide.

As for the flattering imitation of Sibelius, it is enough to say that no composer of symphonies to-day could (none should be) be unaware of that great corpus of Finnish music, whether he admires it (as the English do) or neglects it (as the Germans and French do). The influence of Sibelius upon contemporary composers I am not here called upon to assess. But I have found but little trace of that influence during my study of Vaughan Williams's D major. Maybe there is some central Sibelian principle of symphonic writing, though it would seem to be so elusive as to have passed through the filter of even Mr Cecil Gray's acute analysis. The sole point of resemblance that I can detect between the Finn and the Englishman is that each of them has, in his own way, evolved a symphonic manner individual to himself, by the process of devising from within his own mind a new symphonic method for each major conception. By the similar process of walking, each along his different path, the two composers have arrived at entirely different destinations. The divergences are surely obvious. Thus, for example, Mr Cecil Gray writes of Sibelius;

> From first symphony to last one finds a steady, consistent diminu-
> tion in the use of contrapuntal devices, culminating in the Seventh,
> in which no trace of *fugato* and singularly little polyphony even of
> the freest kind are to be found.

But the symphonies of Vaughan Williams are progressively polyphonic in texture (*cf.* the *passacaglia* here). Mr Gray, again, comments on Sibelius's

> consistent avoidance of thematic connexion between the move-
> ments. . . . After toying tentatively with this device in his First
> Symphony, he then resolutely discarded it and henceforth uncom-
> promisingly maintained the structural integrity of all the separate
> movements.

But in the D major Vaughan Williams firmly attaches scherzo to *Romanza* by a strong thematic coupling, and makes the coda of the finale an epilogue to the whole work by direct quotation from the first movement. And, as a final word on this subject, one might add that, while the style of the D major is so broad as to avoid mannerism, it could not have been achieved by anyone who had not earlier written the *Pastoral* and a number of the other of his most personal works.

The influence of Bunyan, on the other hand, comes more readily to the eye and ear of anyone who regards the music against the background of English life and literature. Direct evidence of unusually close attachment to *The Pilgrim's Progress* was given in the "pastoral episode" of 1922; a kind of associative musical style was created that is the core to Vaughan Williams's expressive mind. Looking backward from that date, we can see the Bunyan association in the *Tallis Fantasia*, forward in works as diverse as *Sancta Civitas*, *Job*, and this Symphony. Even without that first ray of guiding light from the lantern of the composer's handwriting, now darkened by the shutter of print, a listener with some knowledge of his works might have guessed the Bunyan influence. There is, of course, no programme, no direct allusion; any attempt at identification of theme or episode with character or incident would be foolish and profitless. Each of us must see his own *Bild* in the music, not hazard guesses at the composer's. For myself, I see in the D major very little of Mr Worldly Wiseman or of Vanity Fair, and a large amount of Christian against the landscape of those Delectable Mountains. The devil whose laughter cackled "like thorns under a pot" in the F minor, who crashed down the steps, a beaten foe, in *Job*, has here become a mere symbolic figure, an icon of evil, no longer a brilliant, vital tempter. Others will see other visions, visions of their own mind, in this unobjective music. The visual pictures first appearing before the mind's eye as a man hears a new work are not easily taken down from the walls of the mind's gallery. Turn their frames and faces to the wall, relegate them (like the Chantrey Bequest pictures) to the strong-rooms in the cellar, and still those half-pictorial memories persist. Thus, on hearing the *Pastoral* at its first performance, I saw in the scherzo men and women on brief country holiday, with a fairground, and dancing perhaps, a harvest supper, and a jollification on the evening walk back from market day. The composer saw a different *Bild* (he has told me so, though wild horses would not drag from me what he said he himself saw!). Perhaps the most comforting joy of music is that each of us receives it with different, uncommunicable meanings, yet each of us who regards it with honest love is inwardly right. The thoughts contained in great music can be told by one man only—the composer—and only in one way—through his particular music.

Resemblances apart—thematic or associative—to this or that work or the (forthcoming) opera, the influence of *The Pilgrim's Progress* and of Bunyan's mind is sensible. There is more of narrative style in this Fifth Symphony than in the other four. Both formally and in its flow from bar to bar, the music is more loosely wrought—or should I write, 'less firmly controlled'? We are guided, not marched, towards the goal. There is something, too, of Bunyan in the conjunction of youth and age—a superlative achievement in the almost chemical task of making two opposites mix. Never ideological, the composer seems to express here, as Bunyan did in Bedford Gaol, not mere resignation under disaster, but hope during adversity, belief among desert surroundings of steel and salt. The mystical upsurgings of Bunyan's soul have here been re-created into a kind of pantheism, one that has more in it than Bunyan's, and draws its inspiration no less from Blake than from Wordsworth. As a climax of youth in age the D major Symphony stands alone among major works of art.

The indeterminate, though tonal, harmony of the opening chord[1] at once asks a question, which the following phrases

---

[1] The fourth inversion of the dominant seventh, in the key of G major.

do not answer. That, maybe, is a slightly rhetorical opening to the arguments that are to flow from the first doubting phrase. But immediately we feel a sense of space, we are in no confined room around a table, but discussing life in the breadth of the Cotswold air. The long passages of semi-narrative in this first movement do not conflict, in their expression of space, with the succinct, direct utterance, in a few short bars, which is the alleged 'second subject.' This brevity is that of the proverb, not of the epigram; the wisdom of its speech is as old and real as the hills. The outland spaciousness is expanded (not, as usual in argument, contracted) by the development of the first ideas; indeed, our 'second subject' appears even nobler in its return, and the movement as a whole seems to last till eternity—not because of its length, but because of its size and meaning. The rising fourths of the scherzo are characteristic of the composer's hand-work, and so is the drop of the semitone. The fascinating changes of rhythm show a new maturity of development in his speech-rhythm medium of expression. No question is yet answered; we are left, still, to ponder. The *Romanza* hands us a bunch of keys to the door of his soul, but gives us no hint which is the one which will open it. We hark back, here, to "on the beach at night alone," to London's mists, to "the cow looking over the gate," to the rare moments of relief from terror in the F minor. Christian, lonely, stands near us all the time, present but not thinking of companions in his solitary progress. At last, in the *passacaglia* which is the fourth movement, we come upon the warmth of a friendly greeting. Two tunes of equal attraction and of reversed motion are opposed. Then, in the manner of a master who has found freedom in the working of his plastic material, they are played with. A solution to life's problems is given to us; but no one of us receiving the gift can make true use of it unless we give an equal offering out of our inner souls. The coincidence (unnoticed by Vaughan Williams until it was gently put to him) that the resultant curve of the falling upper tune is similar in outline to the German "Easter Hymn" would not be worth a moment's mention, if it were not that in this finale Vaughan Williams attains an universality that overcomes dates and styles, period and fashions. Before he solves each listener's personal problem (if it is soluble in music) he poses his first question once again, and leaves us with many thoughts to help us during this night and many nights to come. The noise of clapping at the end of this Symphony is a vulgar intrusion upon the soul.

Since its first performance on April 21, 1948,[1] musicians have been provided with ample opportunity to become familiar with the sixth of the symphonies, in E minor, by frequent performances and broadcasts under various conductors, and by a handsomely printed semi-miniature score[2] : no similar chance fell to the first four of the Symphonies. Nevertheless, for many the E minor remains still something of an unsolved enigma, not yielding up its meaning as readily as, for example, its predecessor. The proof of this is the flood of explanatory prose which the Symphony has unloosed. The English language, with its genius for the fantastic, abounds in polysyllabic words to describe nonsense. Outside the later music of Scriabin few works of this century have occasioned a greater torrent of poppycock (etc.) than this "challenging symphony" (as it has been called). No doubt, many of the written words were relevant, expository, and (where they had any meaning) true. But as they flood by they leave me convinced that in this music there is something that writers cannot explain, even if they can understand it.

In truth, no explanation is possible. Essentially this Symphony speaks for itself. It is, or it is not—each must decide for himself. But my experience has shown me that among people who deeply love Vaughan Williams's music

[1] Royal Philharmonic Society's Concert, Sir Adrian Boult conducting the B.B.C. Symphony Orchestra.
[2] It is indicative of Vaughan Williams's character that both in his programme notes and in the printed copy he has printed: "The composer wishes to thank Mr Roy Douglas for help in preparing and revising this score."

the E minor rather dams the flow of discussion than opens the sluice-gates.

Vaughan Williams followed his usual practice of writing with his own pen the programme notes for the first performance. In their oddly derisive way they are at once more vague and more illuminating about the music than those he wrote for certain other works—an exposition of what Hardy called "seemings." And so, I personally believe, is the Symphony itself.

The vast size of the symphonic thought is indubitable, though the duration of the music is only thirty-four minutes. As an intellectual feat the Symphony is stupendous for a man of over seventy, though it could hardly have been written by a youngster, however prodigious. Mastery over means of expression has been completely achieved. The composer who found his new-grown self in the D major has allowed the music that is in his soul to manage that self completely. The personality is ruled by the music. In the first five symphonic essays the *materia musica* was contrived to express the thought conceived, invented as the only means of conveying the true meaning of one mind to others. In the sixth the thought seems to grow out of the *materia musica*. The music is dictating to the man, who seems happy to be 'bullied' by his ideas, to be guided by the music itself wherever it elects to take him.

For all its apparent air of positiveness, this Symphony contains, for me, less of direct statement than the others. The epilogue is avowedly inconclusive: "the music drifts about contrapuntally" (runs the composer's note) "with occasional whiffs of theme. . . . At the very end" (he continues after three musical examples) "the strings cannot make up their minds whether to finish in E flat major or E minor. They finally decide on E minor which is, after all, the home key." The scherzo is hardly less unassertive: "fugal in texture but not in structure," the composer calls it, and admits that "various instruments make bad shots at" the "principal subject" before it "settles down." The opening movement is structurally the most complete, with its big melody first in D major and later in E major—so un-Sibelian in its style!

In truth, accepting these "seemings" with grateful mind, I have not yet made up my mind about the weight of this work. At present it appears to me to be less perfect as a work of art, less successful in the fusion of matter and manner, than Three, Four, or Five. It is not a question of his fumbling in the dark to find the way out into the open air. The technical accomplishment is firm and secure—so secure, indeed, that I feel that Vaughan Williams could go on writing music of this same character as long as paper and ink and light and energy lasted. He has mastered the tools, but he shows signs here that they might master him.

Perhaps few of us are old enough to understand the E minor Symphony, perhaps some too old. Perhaps it is for our children and our children's children—if they will listen to it. Perhaps even I shall grow to a proper stature to comprehend its entirety.

No peroration is needed to round off this short study of a great monument of music. Only, one would add, it is with some pleasure that one has observed that the Symphonies—even the *Pastoral*—have been steadily creeping these last few years into the restricted repertoire of our English concert-halls, so saturated with Beethoven and Tchaikovsky.

9

The Choral Works and the "Serenade to Music"

IN the eighteen-seventies to the nineteen-hundreds the
English composer was forced to regard the voice as his
first musical medium. Orchestras were rarities, associated in
'modern' composition with the rival Wagner and Brahms,
and mostly conducted by foreigners. But, prospects of
performance apart, Vaughan Williams's natural instincts as
a composer began with the Englishman's desire to sing. He
approached the goal of music along the conjoining corridors
of voice and verse. After the first important phase of creation
his mind became more and more attuned to the instrumental
medium; in maturity the symphonist *pur sang* emerged out
of that not-very-young-man who was at one time, it seemed,
a thinker in terms of pure poetic, vocal sound. His catalogue
of works (p. 204 *et seq*) shows that the later choral works
occur at dwindling intervals.

And yet the instrumental writing is always coloured by
vocal aspiration. A desire for vocal and linguistic freedom
of rhythm has never deserted Vaughan Williams. We must
observe the other side of the medal. He has increasingly
grown to regard voices as instruments—not quite as Delius
did, for Delius added the tone of the voices as one more
colour to his already laden palette. That is a painter's trick
to which Vaughan Williams was never prone. Voices are,
to him, vibrant living utterances, even when he treats them
instrumentally. But so, for major purposes, he does treat
them.

Of the later choral works one or two might stake a claim

to a position equal to that of the symphonies; others are good, jolly works that every one enjoys singing and hearing —comfortable outbuildings to house casual guests. The choral style is massive and resonant. Deriving from Parry, this choral music, even when unimportant, usually sounds much fuller than Parry's music. The choral works, in a word, 'come off'; in sound they are successful, if not always in meaning. The ear, if not the mind, is pleased.

The best vantage-point for a survey is that noble piece *Sancta Civitas*.

The Latin title was an unfortunate necessity. Arthur R. Gaul had, years before, written a *Holy City*, which had become an annual favourite in Ebenezers and silly little choral societies. The title also misleads. For the English people have the reputation of being insular, people who take their country and their habits abroad with them. History shows the opposite. We English have, in truth, a rare capacity for absorbing the thoughts, the words, the ways, of foreigners; we can digest this alien material and re-express it as English-born. Out of 'transalpine music' we made the very English madrigal, and we cozened Handel, in *Messiah*, into writing music universally accepted as more typically English than that of our own Purcell.

Was there ever, one ponders, a greater translation than that of the 'Revisers'—the anonymous divines of 1611? The Bible is our most English book. Malory and Urquhart cannot compete with them. *The Revelation of St John the Divine* offers us a new English poetry. The first metaphysical vision, full of Eastern colouring and allusion and pictorial reference, was re-created into something that the English people could see with their bare eyes. As the carol-singers brought the Nativity into their own villages and orchards and paddocks, so the 'Revisers' brought the Heavenly City, with all its chrysoprases and sapphires and un-Nordic sunlight, into the home, the parlour. The New Jerusalem could be with us in mind, even if it were not among "those dark Satanic mills."

This astonishing English poem—which was not St John's—Vaughan Williams has built up anew in sound in *Sancta Civitas*. English mysticism is not quite as difficult to understand as it is to define. To those who do not understand, translation is of little value; Donne was never straightforward in his ideas or his language, and even the lucid mind of Milton did not always succeed in making clear his religious thought. Vaughan Williams climbed to the Miltonic height of mystical expression up the Herbert stairway. James Sutherland has pointed out[1] that it is the Englishman's taciturnity to his neighbours, his lack of small talk, that have made English poetry. "From this deep well," Sutherland writes, "hidden from the sight of other men and only dimly apprehended by himself, the Englishman draws his poetry." Professor Westrup puts the point more tersely and appositely: "English music," he writes, "is inclined to be romantic but reserved." The religious tensity of *Sancta Civitas* is at white-hot pitch of temperature, but it is neither fervid nor feverish. Secret and personal, it is also as calmly dignified as *Paradise Lost*.

The simplicity of thought is magnificent, though the physical expression is elaborate, with large forces. A text put together by Vaughan Williams is drawn from chapters xvii, xviii, xix, xxi, and xxii of the Authorized Version of the Revelation, with some additions from Taverner's Bible and the *Sanctus* from the Communion service. Prefatory comes a quotation from the *Phædo* of Plato—that dialogue in which Socrates on his deathbed discourses on the immortality of the soul. The orchestra requires triple wood-wind, including a double bassoon, but without bass clarinet: there is a piano among the percussion instruments. In addition to the baritone solo and the full choir, a semi-chorus of about twenty voices is directed to sit behind the full choir, and as well, out of sight, a distant choir with a separate conductor, which (the composer says) "should consist of boys' voices if

---

[1] In *The Character of England* (ed. Sir Ernest Barker) (Oxford University Press, 1947: "Literature").

possible." Placed alongside this distant choir is one of the three trumpets.

This battalion of workers helps Vaughan Williams to erect a huge cathedral of sound, one that has, for me, an overwhelming beauty. He builds it, as it were, in layers or tiers, piling choir on choir not only to achieve a massive loudness—though there are some mighty climaxes—but also to find remoteness and peace. Through all the tissue of sound comes the personal voice of the composer, intimately telling us the vision he has seen.

In print the work is labelled "oratorio." Anything less like Handel's oratorios, or that long list of 'festival' works that led to the popular decadence of *Penitence*, *Pardon*, *and Peace*, could be imaginable only by another Vaughan Williams. *Sancta Civitas* bears much the same relationship to the traditional Three Choirs, Birmingham-Festival oratorios as do the paintings of El Greco to those of Angelica Kauffmann, or the ceilings of Michelangelo to a well-designed Christmas card. There is, in truth, more than a little of El Greco in this choral work, though the composer may not be aware of it—an angularity of draughtsmanship and design, a dramatic use of unexpected colour. We do not find here the warm, smooth curves of Raphael, the bountiful glow of Andrea del Sarto. Instead there is a stark squareness of pattern, though the music itself is as fluid as speech.

Sancta Civitas needs no further analysis. To attempt to 'explain' it in words, or even on the piano, would be to essay an impertinent parody. It is one of the great mystical works for chorus and orchestra; it jostles in commonalty with the *St Matthew Passion* and Beethoven's Mass in D. It stands no nearer to Elgar's *Dream of Gerontius* than it does to Berlioz's *L'Enfance du Christ*. Absolute in both musical and religious conception, it yet forms a part of the pattern of Vaughan Williams's and of our lives.

Flos Campi speaks to us with something of the same mystical afflatus—ecstatic, feverless, rich, contemplative. In every other way the two works stand contrasted. *Sancta Civitas* may be roughly compared to the frescoes adorning a chancel; *Flos Campi* resembles rather a series of small panels, in the form of a double triptych. One of his most original, and most important, expressions, *Flos Campi* has a strange concatenation of qualities: universal yet personal in speech, unappealing, it is endearing in its beauty; personal in the extreme, it is remote; intimate, it stands in a lone philosophic attitude of thought. To call *Flos Campi* out of the ordinary is a meiosis.

There is no doubt that *Flos Campi* was written, at the importunate pleas of Lionel Tertis for support for his instrument as a soloist, in the form of a piece for a viola-player. The form, on the other hand, did not work out that way; the instrument's sound led to other thoughts, already simmering in the composer's mind (for who knows how long?). The time and the place and the loved one came together, but the nuptials produced this quite astonishing issue. The viola, singing its long line of melody and arabesque, is supported by a choir of singers, who imitate their leader by intoning sounds without words. There should not, we are instructed in the score, be more than twenty to twenty-six singers, but we are given liberty to vary the disposition of these forces within short limits. Nor must we have more than single wood-wind and brass players (two men working *la batterie*), and a "maximum quota" of twenty-two string-players. So accurately is the sound planned that these delicate forces tell us (as van Eyck did) the complete story in the creator's mind at that moment of conception, in full aural realization.

Yet, withal, each of the six panels is prefaced by a verbal quotation, in two languages, from *The Song of Songs*, which is known in the Old Testament as *The Song of Solomon*—first the A.D. 400 Hieronymian Latin from the Vulgate, second the seventeenth-century poetry of the 'Revisers.' The oddity of the thing is that the vocalizers on 'ah' or 'ooh' give us a refracted impression of the words quoted before

each of the pictures. They enounce no intelligible consonants, refer tó no associative logotypes; but they tell us in a
quaint and vague new musical language of the meaning of
their prefaces. The aural values of every note are delicately
balanced, for *Flos Campi* is an exquisite study in pure sound.
The moods are 'realized' with no less delicacy, each subtle
shade of the composer's tonal conception being given full
value in the low scale of colours he has chosen for his medium.
We stand with him, in a rapture of contemplation, on a
lonely island of music, mist-surrounded, though we have,
for ourselves, the dim, mystical light of his music to guide
our feet when we wish to move. Yet, all the while, we are
aware of an unseen ferry, hidden in the enveloping cloud,
which takes us in mind to the *Five Mystical Songs*, to the
Pastoral Symphony, to the *Tallis Fantasia*, or on a voyage into
future discovery to *"Dives and Lazarus"* and the ports of
the D major Symphony.

How this strange, exquisite, integral work came to be
written, on such a subject and at such a date (1925), is
matter for thought for each student of Vaughan Williams's
mind, to be explained, or accepted unexplained but with
gratitude, as we each of us think of that mind. For myself,
I consider its position in the mind's expression central—a
given factor—and the difficulty would appear to me to be
rather to relate other facets of that expression into ocular
and aural relation to this one. Not that I find myself at all
clear, from this wordless musical contemplation, what
exactly is Vaughan Williams's philosophic attitude to that
Oriental erotic collection of poems which the Church has
chosen to expound with an allegorical theology. No two
people think alike on this point. Mr Frank Howes's deep
analysis leads us to believe the composer had an Eastern
imagery in mind. Another commentator (verbally, to me)
has seen in it a commingling of Catholic (and especially
Roman Catholic) Christianity and the Jewish faith. That he
has etherealized the epithalamic poetry, has expressed a love
that partakes more of *charis* than of passion, I do not doubt.

I am content: give me the sound of *Flos Campi*, and if I hear in it a different meaning, see in it a different angle towards the inspiring poetry, I shall like it the more, not the less, for that, each time I hear it.

Built on more slender lines, more delicate in response to the helmsman even than *Flos Campi*, Vaughan Williams's *Magnificat* sails out before us as a splendid, full-rigged ship. In registration it is again an odd piece—contralto solo (Miss Astra Desmond's), female chorus, and orchestra, with a solo flute taking the rôle of evangelist. The design—that is, the musical and literary perception—of this setting of the *Magnificat* is, like *Flos Campi*, exceptional. It has, once again, ecstasy in austerity; but the ecstasy here is different. The text of the canticle is embellished with passages from the Annunciator's greeting and other verses from St Luke's Gospel, which add a remotely dramatic touch to this unliturgical setting of the words. The exquisite English text is handled with a tenderness and a personal love that reflect the deep influence on Vaughan Williams from childhood—one almost feels before, in his progenitors—of the English Church, the English language, and the English Bible. The musical approach to the Virgin's Song of exaltation and humble gratitude is entirely feminine; the composer's music sings the woman's words, as they came from her heart.

For all its innately English quality, for all that it contains of love and faith, with "Philip Sparrow" also sung by contralto solo and women's chorus, *Five Tudor Portraits* makes as wide contrast with the *Magnificat* as any two works by one composer could. This "choral suite in five movements" was written for the Norwich Festival of 1936; the composer conducted it there, and Sir Adrian Boult first gave it to London four months later, in January 1937. It comes, therefore, from the period of the composer's high maturity, and, importantly, represents that maturity. The recalcitrant and jocular Rector of Diss, in Norfolk, John Skelton (1460–1529), educed out of Vaughan Williams all that was music-

ally best in his Englishry. Skelton's was a vivid pen; he
could express, in full-blooded richness, the rumbustious
humour, the poetic fantasy, the triumphant glories, and the
poignant sorrows of the sixteenth century. Skelton's feet
are firmly planted on the English island; his mental flights
of fancy, however freakish, are always within reach of human
hand; his words, however jingly, will always run pat off the
human tongue. The rugged and satiric humour, so clear in
its observation of and sympathy with human frailties, has no
parallel after the poetry of the late Elizabethans. Matching
this early verse with music, Vaughan Williams has shown a
modern outlook; he bridged the gulf of the years with
literal firmness.

The 'choral suite' and the Shakespeare opera *Sir John in
Love* are obviously scions of the same stock; but, despite the
unmistakable family resemblance, they differ in many points,
not only of structure and style, as one would expect of their
differing mediums, but also in the resultant expression of
musical thought. *Five Tudor Portraits* could hardly have
been written by a musician who had not turned his mind to
dramatic music; *Sir John in Love*, of necessity, is narrative
in style, and, as Shakespeare does in *The Merry Wives*,
builds its drama with the bricks of the story—unless one
might prefer to say, "tells the story by means of dramatized
incidents"! This flowing narrative manner which Vaughan
Williams had learned to use with ease and clarity in the
opera is not to be found in the choral work, which, for formal
reasons, has to be more closely argued and balanced in its
several musical patterns. Nevertheless, that acquired narrative power informs the later work, and despite the choral and
orchestration elaborations, Skelton seems to speak his
rattling lines to us with a single individual voice.

To call this impressive piece 'characteristic' of the composer really means, in his case, that it combines under the
one cover of the score a large number of the many varied
qualities combined in his personality. For example, here may
be found many of Vaughan Williams's personal tricks of

idiom; his fingerprints, in combination, make a new pattern —for *Five Tudor Portraits*, though the composer allows us, in his prefatory note, to perform each movement separately, is an integral work of art. Then we find once again here that high literary sense of words in their relation to music which Vaughan Williams inherited from the English tradition. His prefatory note confesses that he has

> ventured to take some liberties with the text. In doing this I am aware [he continues] that I have laid myself open to the accusation of cutting out somebody's 'favourite bit.' If any omissions are to be made, this, I fear, is inevitable. On the whole, I have managed to keep all my own 'favourite bits.'

He has, with his innate sense of reverent musical selection, "occasionally changed the order of the lines." He has interpolated "a song from 'Magnificence'" in *Jolly Rutterkin*. All this is 'characteristic'—very like the man, that is, and the composer within him!

Of the five numbers in the Suite I may shortly comment (for it is an important work) that *The Tunning of Elinor Rumming* is one of Vaughan Williams's highest technical achievements, for it jumbles Skelton and himself without any abrasion of elbows or ankles. *Pretty Bess* (II) is exactly described as an "intermezzo"; a new charm appears here, somewhat gritty, perhaps, as Skelton's verses are! *The Epitaph on John Jayberd of Diss* (III) is, again, precisely entitled "Burlesca," and the humour is Skelton's in the musical tongue of to-day. In V, *Jolly Rutterkin*, Vaughan Williams develops his galumphing sense of the scherzo that blew us about with the "sea-ships" in the nineteen-hundreds and with the threat of war in the nineteen-thirties. It is riotous, violent, boisterous, and extremely difficult to perform with accuracy and clarity, and it has an ancient, broad, un-puritanized humour. There remains IV—one's dear Sparrow; and if I write with sentiment it is because, through this great man's music, I feel I have made a new but lifelong friend of the dear singing lady—Mistress?

L

Lady? Scroop—and her little pet, whom her cat, "Gib," killed; who is compared to "the bird of Araby" and "the Swan of Mæander," and whose soul, she prays, "the Lord will rescue," as she bids him "Farewell, without restore." We climb, easily, the high hill among the range.

The *Six Choral Songs* of 1940—smaller in physical dimensions, but equally large, if anything larger, in mental conception—earn a position of importance. The simple lay-out is for unison voices, of any calibre, and orchestra, or piano; organ would make an equally effective support. The songs bear the sub-title "To be sung in time of war," but in truth they were seldom sung—indeed, strangely neglected —in the war period; the sub-title proves a handicap to-day, and is a misnomer. I should prefer to call them "Songs of Reconstruction," for they look into the future. Shelley's words come from an earlier age of international conflict, from the uneasy times of the opening of the last century. Each of the six is given a title by the composer—a song of "Courage," "Liberty," "Healing," "Victory," "Pity, Peace, and Love," and of "The New Age."

These moral elements, inseparable from war, are no less components of peace; a sage once wrote that "it is easier to die for one's country than live for it." A key to Vaughan Williams's thoughts about Shelley is to be found in the last song, a setting of the words "The world's great age begins anew." True or not, of then or now, those words are the reverse of 'escapism.' Victory is not for Vaughan Williams (or Shelley) a matter of jubilant triumph, but one of responsibility:

> To forgive wrongs darker than death or night,
> To defy Power, which seems omnipotent;
> To love, and bear; to hope till Hope creates
> From its own wreck the thing it contemplates;
> Neither to change, nor falter, nor repent;
> This . . . is to be
> Good, great and joyous, beautiful and free;
> This is alone Life, Joy, Empire, and Victory.

The music is bare, simple, and direct; the words are declaimed with clarity and precision; the mental scale is the immensity of simple faith. I can think of nothing more impressive than a thousand unpolished voices spontaneously joined in singing this stark and noble music. Here, if ever such was, is music of and for the people, without relation to time or event.

Thanksgiving for Victory stands, in my view, at the head of several less important works for chorus and orchestra. The text, chosen by the composer, is expressive of a true religious thankfulness. "Violence shall be no more heard in thy land, wasting nor destruction within thy borders; but thou shalt call thy walls Salvation, and thy gates Praise." Patriotic feeling is symbolized in Kipling's simple hymn to the Motherland, "Land of our birth, we pledge to thee Our love and toil in the years to be."[1] There is a total absence of jubilation over the conquered, always a humble but strongly creative desire for service for the future betterment of mankind. "O God" (he quotes from *Henry V*) "thy arm was here And not to us, but to thy arm alone Ascribe we all. Take it, God, for it is none but thine." The remainder of the text is drawn from *The Song of the Three Holy Children*, and from the books of 1 Chronicles (xxix) and Isaiah (lx–lxii).

"This work," we read in a foreword, "was originally designed for broadcasting. For Church and concert use certain modifications are necessary." The first elaborate lay-out, directed towards reproduction through the microphone, used considerable forces; a soprano solo (to be "sung by a powerful dramatic voice, but there must be no vibrato"), a speaker (whose voice must "absolutely dominate" the accompanying music), a children's choir (which "must be sung by real children's voices, not sophisticated choir boys"), chorus (with baritones singing either a fifth line or supporting the tenors, of whom Vaughan Williams complains in his note of "the chronic scarcity"), and large

[1] From *Puck of Pook's Hill*.

orchestra, including six trumpets, sixteen clarinets, and doubled timpani. A 'cued in' version makes the work available for an ordinary symphony orchestra, with organ and one or two other instruments *ad libitum*.

Never one who cared to write to order (nor easily could, for he has but little of the *ad hoc* journalist in him), Vaughan Williams has produced in *Thanksgiving for Victory* a magnificent work of art—noble as well as moving, with both grandeur and simplicity. Its self-contained success is testimony to the complete command of *materia musica* that he has acquired through years of struggle and self-direction. If in its sixteen minutes' duration the work has not the profundity of thought or the mystical ecstasy of *Sancta Civitas* and some of the Symphonies, it stands as a worthy companion and successor to them.

The same high praise can hardly be awarded to the larger *Dona Nobis Pacem*, which was written for the centenary of the Huddersfield Choral Society and performed by that body under Albert Coates in 1936. A large work, this cantata is designed for soprano and baritone soli, chorus, and orchestra; with text taken from a variety of sources—an ancient liturgical prayer in Latin that gives the work its title, three poems (in part) by Walt Whitman, the famous "Angel of Death" speech of John Bright, and passages (with some adaptation) from the biblical books of Jeremiah, Daniel, Haggai, Micah, Leviticus, Psalms, Isaiah, and St Luke. There is nothing here of the fresco-like quality of *Sancta Civitas*; despite a certain nobility, it is openly a "tract for the times," and, like so much propaganda, it defeats its own ends (rather nobly). To the student of Vaughan Williams's musical style and growth the score is interesting, for (in the words of Mr Frank Howes) "it is a compilation of pieces written at two different periods but strung together on the thread provided by the title." The *Dirge for Two Veterans* takes us back to the Whitman phase.

So we come to the smaller, one might say jollier, slighter pieces, some written for the Leith Hill Festival. Of these the *Benedicite* is the most interesting, *In Windsor Forest* (adapted from *Sir John in Love*) the most engaging. All may be profitably read as studies in texture, and not one is of mediocre quality.

There remains the *Serenade to Music*. It absolutely refuses to be classified or categorized, and would deserve a chapter to itself if words could do anything to illuminate its exquisite and transparent glow of beauty.

Sir Henry Wood, for the gift which Vaughan Williams was to present to him for his Jubilee as a conductor in 1937, made a strange and exacting request; one, however, which could not but appeal to the democratic humanity of the composer. Wood wished that the new work might contain a contributory part for each of sixteen well-known singers who had been associated with his concert life. With (I fancy) some misgivings, but with apparent ease in the result, Vaughan Williams tackled this singular problem in a separate way—the direct way of writing a work, literally, for sixteen soloists and orchestra, without supporting chorus, the choral chording being provided by the soloists themselves. The words he took from the opening of the last act of *The Merchant of Venice*. The permission given by the composer in his printed directions that the work may be sung by choir and (if it must be) four single soloists may have brought the work into a wide and lasting range of performance. To those who heard it first, on the other hand, such compromise is almost artistic sin.

The recipe for compounding the extraordinary philtre which is the *Serenade* is not to be discovered by a common critic's analytical laboratory. Some elements will lie dormant—in what quantity?—like Shakespeare's verses, love for Sir Henry Wood, the unusualness of the vocal medium, the time and circumstances of the composer's life. However dispensed, this music stands isolated as a single work among the whole of Vaughan Williams's large catalogue. It is perhaps the most successfully integrated, the most concordant, the sweetest on the ear, of all his inventions, matter and manner indissolubly fused. He has distilled a new beauty out of "the touches of sweet harmony"—his own beauty, but a different one from those many visions of the elusive virtue he has expressed elsewhere. Dulcitude is not all, however; with his inborn dramatic sense Vaughan Williams has gently and with kindly humour portrayed in their several solos the characters of the singers' voices. For Elsie Suddaby a part differing from that for Eva Turner; a differentiation between Norman Allin and Harold Williams. Let us admit that in the long stretch of time these amiable *badinages* will have no meaning. Yet æsthetically they lend colour and character to the vocal parts, leavening the texture of the whole. Such music will not soon blossom again.

IO

Other Instrumental Works

AMONG the orchestral[1] and chamber pieces remaining
for consideration, perhaps the most important, certainly
the most interesting, is *Five Variants of "Dives and Lazarus,"*
for string orchestra and harp, the violas and violoncellos
being divided each into two voices and the harp to be
"doubled if possible." Thirty years separate it from the
Fantasia on a Theme by Thomas Tallis, for "*Dives and
Lazarus*" was first performed under Sir Adrian Boult at the
New York World's Fair in 1939, when the composer was
sixty-seven years of age. A family likeness between the
two works can hardly escape notice. "*Dives and Lazarus*"
is a side-piece, lying off the beaten track; it is no obvious
"great masterpiece," as *Job* was acclaimed to be from the
first. But "great men" (we learn from *Bleak House*) "have
their poor relations," and Longfellow corrected certain
common views when he wrote, "The heights by great men
reached and kept were not attained by sudden flight."
The tune "*Dives and Lazarus*" is an English folk-carol
that has been found in many parts of the country in differing
forms. Its origin none knows, but its antiquity may be
judged by the mention of it as a familiar "merry ballad"
in 1619 in John Fletcher's play *Monsieur Thomas* (printed
1639). Continuing in popularity during the eighteenth
century, it survived in oral memory up to recent times. In
direct but coloured rustic verse the parable of the rich and
poor men, as first recounted in the Gospel according to St
Luke, chapter xvi, is told to us by the singer as if it were
happening to-day in his own village, with local detail. The

[1] *Job* is properly relegated to the next chapter.

167

melody itself appears in the *Oxford Book of Carols* in the form noted down by the late A. J. Hipkins (oddly enough in Westminster); but another version is printed in that book taken from the singing of Mr John Evans, far away in Dilwyn, and texts from various sources.

At this point the composer's note preceding the score is important: he writes, "These variants are not exact replicas of traditional tunes, but rather reminiscences of various versions in my own collection and those of others." We are thereby forewarned that this is a musing work, music that contains the dreams and memories of a folk-song collector, music that expresses the soaring soul rather than the plain substance of the folk-song, the music of England, in a word, as re-expressed by a great and sympathetic Englishman. 'Variants,' not variations, is the proper designation.

The tune is first fully stated in its 4/4 version; then, in Variant I, in 3/4, the treatment is antiphonal, with the harp in an important position. Variant II is quicker and bolder, with less for the harp to do. A solo violin appears in Variant III with a new modal version of the theme, based on the chord of D minor, while the violas lead IV, in 2/4 time and marked "l'istesso tempo." The last variant is rich and full in sound, reaching a big climax, whereupon a solo 'cello has its say with the tune, and the work ends on long, peaceful chords.

No such height of mystical glory is reached in the later work, maybe, as irradiates with its rarefied light the earlier *Tallis Fantasia*. The two informing melodies are not equally sublime, though in idiom they are related in the way that Angelo's verse is akin to Mistress Quickly's prose. On the contrary side, "*Dives and Lazarus*" is written with an expressive power which, even in that profound younger work about Tallis—work of projective genius though it is— the composer had not then solved. The point is concerned with more than musical technique, with, also, artistic accomplishment. In the later, Vaughan Williams has arrived at a new level of expression, a fresh but long-learnt power of controlling his note-heads to give his full sounded meaning. The result is that "*Dives and Lazarus*" is a deeply significant piece of music.

The virtuoso soloist, in his kaleidoscopic guise in the concert hall, has never been a figure to attract Vaughan Williams, who has tended, in his musical preference, towards the amateur, towards the communal music-maker finding his pleasure in a part in the choir or, as a player, in the back desks of the second violins accompanying a choral piece. Though to more than one movement Vaughan Williams has affixed the title *Romanza*, he is in truth no 'Romantic,' in the accepted nineteenth-century sense. If Bach, Purcell, Byrd, were Romantics, then we may extend the ordinary word to include our own composer. When he deals with soloists Vaughan Williams is apt to ask them to play instrumental tropes and melismas that have more musical meaning than public effectiveness. His flourishes are not those of the *improvisatore*, but those of the thinker. He prescribes action, directed towards the aim of musical intention.

Two concertos for soloist with orchestra are extant, that for violin and that for oboe. The Piano Concerto I regard as a symphony.

When Vaughan Williams wrote the *Concerto Accademico*[1] (1925) he was in his early fifties, and was going through a phase of great creative invention, and a strong determination to express himself in an English musical language suited to his immediate needs. I myself do not believe entirely in 'reactions' in composers, as they are talked about nowadays. There is as serious a difference in meaning between *Sancta Civitas* and the *Concerto Accademico* as there is between their two mediums of expression and the expressive meaning behind them. I will concede, somewhat reluctantly and without a trace of personal information, that the Concerto shows the influence of Gustav Holst. A better phrase would be 'kinship of mind at this moment of life'; I am incapable of seeing any other influence (of technical tricks the one

[1] Now re-entitled Concerto in D minor for violin and strings.

taught the other I have no cognizance) in any other work by Vaughan Williams, and here I feel he was, in fact, far ahead mentally of Holst. He shared but little save personal love with the latter's seemingly direct but actually tortuous mind.

In many ways it would be true to say that the *Concerto Accademico* offers us a small epitome of Vaughan Williams's instrumental style at the moment of the mid-nineteen-twenties. Absolute music at its barest—even though one theme in the finale is acknowledged as "in part, taken from the composer's opera, *Hugh the Drover*"—the score shows in every bar a clear sign-manual. The word *Accademico* caused (but need cause no more) a misapprehension at the first hearings. The implication is not derogatory, as 'academic' (a word of different meaning in our modern world) is used in England: only that the form derives from the eighteenth-century concertos of Bach and his fellows.

The idiom is as unadorned as a rake, the scoring as angular and purposeful as a farm tractor—open fifths for the fiddler and strings of triads for the rest of the players. There is no attempt at sweetness of sound. This is muscular music, without spare flesh or comfortable curves; lean, virile, and athletic. There is much rhythmic playing with the ideas, and the arabesques in the second movement (where also a plain scale is an important idea) are a decoration of the Bach type, suggestive of carved stone rather than of surface colour. After one concession to tenderness of sound the presto succeeds the adagio in an elaborate pattern, splashed before us at a headlong pace.

The Oboe Concerto (1944) is no gentler, but more mature. There is more exploitation of the soloist, for whom is written an extremely difficult part.[1] Again following the older *Grosso* in a modern shape, the oboe work relies upon the salient characteristics of the solo instrument—in this case, the spitting, spiky tone, the sharp-sounding trills, and the long holding notes. The musical speech is terse and

[1] I was unable to go to Liverpool to hear the first performance, but I hazard the guess, "from information received," that the printed score has been edited, in some ways reduced (shall we say?), by Mr Léon Goossens, C.B.E.

direct, with a good measure of humour. A cadenza in the
tenth bar tells us, quite firmly, that the soloist is present and
dominating. A minuet is somewhat rustic in style. All this
semi-contrapuntal discussion leads us to an epilogue, in G
major, where the texture is richly woven in the warm colours
of an Aubusson carpet. But the acid jocularity of the oboe
has a further say, and the work ends, somewhat curiously,
on a soloist's top D (pianissimo, if he can), with a pleasant
string chord below in G major.

Of less interest but more readily accepted by the ear is
the Viola Suite written for Lionel Tertis to play in 1934.
The music, laid out on an original plan, is scored for small
orchestra to support the soloist, with only one oboe among
the double wood-wind, two horns, two trumpets, no trombones, and celesta among the percussion; but it was also
published as a suite for viola and pianoforte, the composer's
intention clearly being to make the work ready to the hand
of the home-player and student. The plan, above mentioned,
groups the eight pieces into three sections—I Prelude,
Carol, and Christmas Dance, II Ballad and Moto per-
petuo, III Musette, "Polka Mélancolique," and Galop.
Section III approximates nearest to the traditional suite-
idea; the other two sections are more arbitrary in their
choice of expressional forms. The work has an odd kind of
open-air tang to it, a fresh quality unusual in music designed
for a virtuoso player. Though in fact no single folk-tune is
used as a theme, the music gives us a feeling of the natural
styles of the people—not only in the narrative 'Ballad' but
also in the other pieces. It is pleasant rather than important.

The incidence of viola tone in Vaughan Williams's works,
over a long period, cannot be missed by those who have ears.
In his last chamber-piece it takes the lead. The Second
String Quartet, in A minor, is directed by the composer to
be entitled, in programmes, with its second line, "For Jean
on her birthday." The "Jean" was, of course, the daughter
of the late Dr H. C. Stewart, who, athlete at all times (he
played cricket for Kent, and was a 'blue,') was music-master

at Tonbridge School, Kent, before he took on the organist-
ship of Magdalen College, Oxford. The work was first
played in 1945.

Earlier attempts at chamber music come to mind—the
String Quartet, for example, written (or performed?) in
1908, and revised in 1921. The scherzo is clearest in my
memory, for it is characteristic of the composer. Most of the
other music I seem to have heard better expressed in later
works. Perhaps the *Fantasy Quintet*, written about 1910, is
a better work—I do not know—with its two violas and
resultant middle-pitch tones.

The A minor String Quartet is pleasing to read and to
listen to: it is not a major work, but mature and convenient,
once you (the listener) know the Vaughan Williams style.
Mechanical mastery over the medium makes the texture
full and free. There is no effort and little elaboration. The
cross-accentuation is interesting, like the liberty of speech-
rhythm which the composer learnt from the older masters of
the voice. In the first movement the flow of the music is
wayward, but at times queerly passionate: the tonal melisma
is full, at once, of vigour and emotion. The G minor
"Romance" employs both contrapuntal and chordal devices.
The phrase that opens the scherzo is labelled as a borrowing
from his film-music to *49th Parallel*. An epilogue—once
again—displays the mind of the long thinker, the ages-old
craftsman in the art of music, which he has learned by the
skill of 'hand-practice' ('ear-practice'? 'conductor-practice'?):
by some recipe that I am incapable of giving in formula
to young composers. Nowhere (not even in the Fifth
Symphony) has Vaughan Williams written music so philosophical, so resigned, so restful in simplicity; the keys of D
and F major bring us home, and there is a beautifully
planned, wholehearted repeat of the final section to take us
to the peace of sleep.

Two works stand undiscussed, apart from the *Charterhouse Suite*—an arrangement made with the help of James
Brown—and two organ pieces, which may, I think, be over-

passed here without offence to anyone. The *Partita* for
strings, produced in the same year as the Sixth Symphony
(1948), began life as a double trio—that is, a divided sextet
—written for Isolde Menges and her associate players in *1938*
~~1925~~: withdrawn, it was rewritten, laid out once more for
two groups of three-part string-players, and launched anew
with a fresh last movement. It is now easy in its technical
production of musical sounds; what it was before we cannot
tell! The texture is engaging, and that in spite, perhaps, of
the fact that the music is earthy. The prelude, kind to the
ear, is meditative, a tranquil movement of beauty, which leads
into a scherzo marked 'ostinato.' The repeated phrase is
short and pert, and obstinately persists through the movement, with a major-key trio as a relief before the return. The
Intermezzo is labelled "Homage to Henry Hall"; in its
unexpected nostalgia and guitar-like accompaniment, with
elaborately not-quite-off-the-dance-floor rhythms, one under-
stands what the composer was aiming at. But there is a
noticeable kinship between the main tune and the slightly
grotesque figure of the scherzo; so arises a suspicion that the
composer's homage was tinged with humour, one way or the
other. The final *Fantasia* is well named—a swift movement
of cross accents and no finality of meaning.

I have never heard *Household Music* (1942) played on any
instruments other than the tender strings for which it was
primarily written. The music sounded ineffably beautiful at
that aural moment, but not, I think, more beautiful than it
does in abstraction, in the inner ear, as one reads and re-reads
the printed score. These "Three Preludes on Welsh Hymn
Tunes" are, in fact, so written that (in his own words) "the
composer has envisaged their being played by almost any
combination of instruments which may be gathered together
in one household." His envisagement of a household
embraces, in its wide survey of human activity, instruments
like the following alternatives: oboe, clarinet, flute, recorders,
soprano or E-flat saxophones, or cornet. E-flat saxhorn,
bassoon, bass clarinet, B-flat saxophone, or euphonium.

What joy to hear—some, all, any of them! But the house-holds I know do not lean towards them, or, if they do, only in the direction of music not so permanent in its appeal.

I end this chapter with this work because it is the crowning achievement of a long life of instrumental writing —not for inner meaning, wide scope, or massiveness of form; we turn to the Symphonies for the large qualities and the important statements, the epic idea and the expression of it in fitly grand terms. Here is a little perfection, beautiful in itself because it comes from a beautiful mind schooled by hard effort to a proper manner of exposition.

II

Music for Stage and Film

FEW operas hold the boards for long; the lists in bibliographies of composers and in Loewenberg make depressing reading. In England fewer new operas have a chance of success than, for example, in the Germany of the 1920–33 period, or the pre-1914 period—fewer, Dr Hans Heinsheimer hopes, than may be produced in modern, youthful, upspringing America.[1] After the first musical William Wallace and M. W. Balfe few Englishmen seem to have kept their audiences. Professor Dent wrote, "The public, in general, is more interested in singers than in composers." *Esmeralda*, by Goring Thomas, Naylor's prize-winning *The Angelus*, Stanford's *Travelling Companion* and *Shamus O'Brien*, not to mention Nicholas Gatty's and Ethel Smyth's, Rutland Boughton's and Delius's pieces, to name but few strugglers in the field—"all, all are gone, the old familiar faces." Britten remains, and the years may condemn.

At the best the musical surveyor tends to regard the operatic tract in the wide lands of any composer's bibliography as so much waste ground—undevelopable, hardly worth the theodolite. With Vaughan Williams the facts are otherwise. His stage-works provide a corpus of music, not as important, perhaps, but in length as cognizable, as the Symphonies and Piano Concerto. They must be known and examined if the pattern of his creative life is to shake itself into proper design. We, as members of the public, may not

---

[1] For an illuminating, but statistically somewhat dubious, account of modern opera I refer the reader to Dr Heinsheimer's book *Menagerie in F sharp*, republished in London by T. V. Boardman and Co., Ltd (1949). It provides good and informative reading.

be allowed to hear them, because of the majority vote of the box-office; privately we may study and learn from them.

An essential but unexplainable element in the compound of this great man is his natural sense of dramatic action and of its reproduction in terms of music. He inherits it from his near progenitors, the Elizabethans. He began to show it early. The Munich visit had a lasting influence. The instinct has not waned, for if, as I write, we have not yet heard (save in a run-through) or seen the 'morality' based on *The Pilgrim's Progress*, which succeeded the Sixth Symphony, we know from the typescript libretto that age cannot wither the dramatic flame. Little room for its burning light was available to the young man in the nineteen-hundreds, and the academic opera of that period came no more readily to his purposes and ambitions than the conventional oratorio or the Mus. Doc. exercise. *A Sea Symphony*, if it contains drama only in the symphonic sense of tense movement, has in it much of dramatization, of people, elements of nature, and poetic images. The *London Symphony*, if my view is accepted, is dramatic in issue, however symphonic in intention. It may not be forgotten that *Hugh the Drover* occupied the composer's thoughts during the same years that were the gestation period of the *London*.

Hugh the Drover is an early venture, a voyage into a new medium that would contain the springing enterprise of this musical explorer. The opera must not be taken as a complete achievement, as more than a happy haven at the end of a first enterprising expedition. Good qualities abound; but I cannot believe that we find in these two acts the veritable or 'central' Vaughan Williams.

Ebullient energy combines with a strong inventive flow to produce an always interesting musical texture. The composer pours tunes over us. The idiom is, for the most part, personal and original, though here and there it lapses into conventionalities of the stage, and even into the musical tricks of others (one can hear Coleridge-Taylor now and then, for example—another man who was stifled by English lack of operatic opportunity). The ensembles are skilfully done if perhaps a little heavy-handed; even in the revised versions not everything is (I will not say audible) intelligible in the simple stage sense. It is all lovable, engaging stuff. And then? One is compelled into a questioning attitude.

There is something of charades about *Hugh the Drover*. The nationalism is fervid but self-conscious. This is English opera, indeed, but that does not mean that it is, even nationally, universal opera, like *The Bartered Bride* or *Boris Godounov*, like *Rigoletto* or *Carmen*. Hugh himself is a Siegfried, a touch mock-heroic, no superman and leader, but a liberator as the free-thinker among the ordinary people. He is to set free English music (and English thought, perhaps, too) from the fire-ringed conventions of Mrs Grundy. Folk-song and folk-dance are used for deliberately picturesque purpose. Hugh, indeed, is so picturesque, with his boxing match, his stocks, his escape, and his love triumphant, as to be unconvincing.

Once more one is forced to comparison with Thomas Hardy. Unfortunately the librettist, Harold Child, despite his close friendship with and writings about that great novelist and poet, was no Hardy. *Under the Greenwood Tree* was described by the author in the sub-title "A rural painting of the Dutch School"; *The Trumpet Major* records domestic events, local to Overcombe, which were contingent upon the threat of Napoleonic invasion. Hardy delved his novels out of a mine of fresh lore, of memories in the minds of his father and of other, longer-lived folk who had heard and seen with their own faculties, or, at worst, whose informants were near and only recently deceased relatives. Harold Child, we feel, had read the archives of, the poems about, that Cotswold village, with its stocks and its fair. And for once—the only occasion in his life that matters to the musical student—Vaughan Williams accepted this charming compromise between literature and life as the real thing, the thing that provided (as, indeed, it did to some extent) the outlet his mind was then seeking. Everywhere else in his

M

stage works Vaughan Williams found means to 'realize' (in the painter's sense) the libretto before him. Here he was forced, partly by the words and partly by his own ideas, to produce *pastiche*. As such it does not convince me.

But this cattle-driving, boxing Siegfried went far to liberate his creator. The influence of Wagner on this consciously English work was odd: it gave the composer a power of writing passionate love-duets in his own style and to English words, literary but hardly impassioned! *Hugh the Drover* is a first big attempt, and as such is, too, an outlet from the oratorio or respectable overture or forgotten symphony, a boon to the composer and so to us. It is a mine of lovely music, of good tunes well presented.

At a remote point in the antipodes of the operatic world stands *Riders to the Sea*, a one-act opera composed in 1926, not published till 1936, and, for certain internal reasons of difficulty, seldom performed, never on a stage more professional than that of a broadcast studio. It is a word-for-word setting of J. M. Synge's play of Irish life with the same title. Synge's naturalistic ambition was to reproduce in verity on the stage the remote Irish peasantry, which, with all its limitations and ignorance, can speak in a language of poetic beauty and flowering imagery. These rich, simple, and unalterable words of Synge's Vaughan Williams has treated not only with faithfulness, but also with an imaginative understanding seldom accorded by a composer to a poet. For the purpose he once again forged a new musical language, suited to no other occasion. In the result we have a tragic music-drama sung to a small orchestra in a continuous recitative—virtually *Sprechstimme* of a new (and English) kind. Certain main motifs represent the sea (a protagonist in Synge's play) and the death of an unknown character, for example, but they are fragmentary, almost shadowy. There is no long melody, and much of the music seems to be a muttering in the shadows of a sorrow-haunted cottage. The chorus parts, wordless throughout, represent the primitive, wailing chant known in Ireland as "keening." The orchestral

texture is slight and dark in colour—for example, the single
clarinet is the bass instrument.

The characters recreated in music by the composer have
strong reality—Maurya the mother, the daughter Nora,
the only surviving son of her three, Bartley. Even the
drowned Patch and the missing Michael, the finding of
whose clothes is an element of the play's action, are shadowed
in. As well, Vaughan Williams has made into living
characters the oppressed atmosphere of the sorrowful house,
the sea that surrounds their lonely island off the Galway
coast, the tragedy of their lives.

No opera written before or since can be quoted in parallel
to this rarely beautiful work of only thirty minutes' extent.
The composer has, one feels, learnt something from
Moussorgsky, with his power of bringing on to the stage, as
if to be seen, the background emotions of his characters and
their intertwined lives. Something, too, he may have
learnt from the one-act opera of his friend Holst—*Savitri*.
In musical method *Riders to the Sea* stands closer to Debussy's
Pelléas et Mélisande, but in all other ways it stands musically
alone. But it stands very close alongside Synge, a perfect
musical counterpart to his literal poetry-in-prose.

Critical but loving examination leads me to believe that
Hugh the Drover is really a sketch for *Sir John in Love*. This
is not critical exaggeration. *Sir John* is, perhaps, to be
described as the fulfilment of *Hugh*'s aspirations. Only five
years separate the two operas in performance, but one dare
suspect that the Falstaff idea had occurred in Vaughan
Williams's mind as a possible subject for opera before the
First World War, when he was talking of Hugh the Boxer
with Harold Child. The second opera is as accomplished in
technique as the first is tentative. But the bold policy adopted
by the composer of using Shakespeare's own text, "this
wonderful comedy," justified itself entirely. Shakespeare's
Merry Wives of Windsor has been much criticized; Falstaff
is not the man he was in Henry IV, the job Shakespeare did
was to please Elizabeth, and so on. I have always thought

the play good, and funny: I think the same of Vaughan Williams's opera. He has translated Shakespeare into English music; but our operatic stage prefers the Italian and German accents.

The reality of Shakespeare's characters is underlined in this work, with a humour real and human, spoken out of the mouths of the people. Less folk-music is used in *Sir John* than in *Hugh*. "When I could not find a suitable folk-tune," writes the composer in a preface,

> I have made shift to make up something of my own. I therefore offer no apology for the occasional use of a folk-song to enhance a dramatic point. If the result is successful I feel justified; if not, no amount of 'originality' will save the situation. However, the point is a small one, since out of a total of 120 minutes' music, the folk-tunes occupy less than 15.

Yet the later opera is expressively English, while the earlier is only consciously, even strivingly, English. Between the composer and his main character there exists a national sympathy—I would not say a friendship, but the loving sympathy of humorous interplay of words and music. I feel, from this score, that Falstaff had been slyly standing at Vaughan Williams's elbow for many long years.

A new flow carries us along in *Sir John*, a narrative style completely attained, a genuineness in the matching of the colours and moods of words with music so that neither clashes. The characterization is exact and entertaining.

I have sometimes wondered, in the thoughts that come during rest in the night, whether the cause of the failure of this lovely opera—warmly romantic at times as well as swift in movement (*e.g.*, in Mistress Quickly's great scene)— whether the cause were not the lack of Englishry in our performing artists and our listening audiences. The only professional production I in person have seen complicated the simple tissue of the work with attempts to be interesting and amusing; the characters, under the producer, would 'play' the piece, instead of letting the big projective movements of the composer carry them along, in all simplicity, to success. Verdi's masterpiece was planned by Boïto: Vaughan Williams's no less great work was directed by Shakespeare's mind, and planned in Vaughan Williams's.

Somewhere, hovering near these two other operas, floats *The Poisoned Kiss*, with the second title of "The Empress and the Necromancer." It is in an entirely different *genre* from Vaughan Williams's other stage works. Openly a comic opera, it has spoken dialogue between the musical 'numbers'; both text and music are often intentionally humorous, dependent upon wit for the audience's laughter; there are burlesque, satire, modern allusions, fairy-tale fantasy, and a lightly entertaining musical style. In fact, *The Poisoned Kiss* is what it is described to be—an extravaganza. But the description includes the qualifying word 'romantic.'

For all this external divagation from the style of the two previous operas, this third work bears a likeness to them; indeed, the differences are less important than the fundamental similarities of musical thought.

Up to now *The Poisoned Kiss* has never been professionally presented; no impresario has risked a halfpenny on it. English though it is through to its vitals, in the great line of *Singspiel* and ballad opera, no provision can be found for it in English musical life, it seems. The Savoy operas absorb what attention our theatre managers pay to light opera of a class better than a kind of highbrow revue. Such pieces are left to the amateurs, if they have the enterprise to discover and undertake them.

The first performances of the opera were, in fact, given by a cast predominantly formed of Cambridge undergraduates, with the principal parts sung by professionals and some stiffening in the chorus. For certain reasons the dialogue was cut, and the audience laughed less often than was intended. In other amateur productions I have seen the text was faithfully followed, to the hilarious delight of every one present.

The humour (if one may dare to hold down for temporary

examination so delicate a specimen as humour) is rich; the situation is funny, the plot entertaining, the dialogue brilliantly apt and well placed. There is no resemblance here to the boisterous larking of the earlier *Wasps* music. Richard Garnett's *Twilight of the Gods* was a set of short stories so novel in their outlook that even *Erewhon* Butler could say the good things about them that he refused to most of English literature, save to the Sonnets of Shakespeare. The libretto was written by Evelyn Sharp, sister of Cecil Sharp, later married to Henry W. Nevinson—a poet, a writer of children's stories, a suffragist, a *Manchester Guardian* journalist—all the points listed above (as they say) qualified her admirably to understand Garnett's cynical humour as he grafted it on to Nathaniel Hawthorne's original bole of an idea. The story of the girl brought up on poisons, through the jealousy of her father, whose kiss would kill her first successful suitor, he happening to be the son of the subject of the father's jealousy, who had brought up her child on antidotes: Evelyn Sharp made of this story no less a moving than an entertaining play, with delightful sub-characters like the three Hobgoblins and the three psychic mediums. Her literary tradition was of the highest, her verses were as nimble as Praed's, as fresh and topical as "Lucio's," or "Evoe's," or "Dum-Dum's." The libretto stands, a solid and well-constructed play. If actors and producers treat the work with a little visual fantasy and ingenuity no one need have fears about the successful reception of either words or music, which, joined, are cumulative in effect.

Musical points of interest abound. Never lacking in fantastic ideas, the score is very closely written—firm on its feet, but not for a moment heavy. The galumphing passages are carefully and ironically planned. In most of the score a new ease and delicacy make their appearance, though the final impression it gives is one of broad and genial robustness. The characters in any extravaganza have to some extent to be labelled with tickets showing their more obvious

characteristics; Miss Evelyn Sharp's sympathetic understanding of human nature can to some extent penetrate
through the characterizing costumes to the person below
each docketed member of the plot. Vaughan Williams adds
to her success by making the characters come musically alive.
The Empress is a case in point; in her late appearance
(Act III) she is not merely a *dea ex machina*, but an intensely
alive contralto. Hob, Nob, and Gob are as real as the
languishing professional mediums. As for the tunes the
singers are given, they jostle one another in their profusion,
but not so roughly that the score seems like an over-rich
cake. Here, surely, we can find those tunes which somehow
we were never quite happy with in *Hugh the Drover*, strong,
full-blooded melodies ranging from tenderness to an ironic
manliness. Nor, because he has set himself out to write
captivating tunes, catchy valses, a semi-serious tango, and a
painfully lifelike sentimental duet in Act III, has Vaughan
Williams surrendered to popular taste one yard of that
territory which is his personal idiom and method of writing
music. Once again we meet the avoidance of set tonic-and-
dominant cadences (especially in the rising bass), the tonal
arabesques, the individual harmonies (*cf*. the opening of
Act II). Even the parodies show the old Adam.

The sub-title says 'romantic'; not even in the music for
Fenton and "sweet Anne Page" has the composer written
more richly, imaginatively, and substantially than in the big
scene between Tormentilla and Amaryllus in Act II.
Romantic feeling pervades the whole opera. But Vaughan
Williams's romance is never nostalgic; it is youthful,
hopeful, projective. The loving couples are, each in their
respective degree, about to sail on a voyage to happiness
without a thought or regret for the past.

Above all, one is conscious throughout *The Poisoned Kiss*
of the immense enjoyment the composer had while writing
it; it is obvious that (as he once confessed privately) he was
writing music he really liked. Far more than gusto is
breathed out from these pages of music: a genuine musical

satisfaction, an almost paternal humour, blow over us from first to last page.

The "Masque for Dancing," *Job*, "founded on Blake's *Illustrations to the 'Book of Job*,'" is unquestionably one of Vaughan Williams's major works, standing musically in an equal importance with certain of the Symphonies and with, for example, *Sancta Civitas* and *Five Tudor Portraits* of the choral-orchestral works. The composing of this noble music was the principal occupation of his mind during the 1929–30 period, and so may be said to represent the full maturity of his second period. The *Benedicite* and two other Leith Hill works are also dated 1930, and the composer was already contemplating his F minor Symphony, though it was not sketched till after *Job* nor performed till 1935. The story of the Masque's origin is, one imagines, well known—how the Blake scholar Dr Geoffrey Keynes projected a ballet based on William Blake's *Job* drawings and offered the idea to Diaghilev; how eventually there were gathered together Ninette de Valois, Gwendolen Raverat, and Ralph Vaughan Williams; how it first appeared as an orchestral suite at the Norwich Festival in October 1930; and how it was produced in full panoply, under Constant Lambert's stick, at the new Camargo Society (founded by the late Lord Keynes, the doctor's brother) in 1931, helping that society and its workers and sponsors in the great task of founding an English school of ballet, now an established institution in our national life at Sadler's Wells and Covent Garden.

As a work of art the full score of *Job* does not live in the isolated musical self-sufficiency of a symphony, of a pattern conceived and created in absolute sound. It is a synthesis of several arts and of several minds. The first conceptions of Dr Keynes were interpreted in dance, visual portrayal, drama, and music by his three closely allied partners. Above them all towered the majestic figure of William Blake, who with mind and pencil poured over them all the philosophy of good and evil that he had distilled from the earlier thoughts of the ancient prophets and from the powerful

English words of the translating divines. Separate the music
from the dance and the décor, play it in a concert hall, and
at once you hide William Blake's piercing light under a
bushel, if you do not snuff it out altogether. The music of
the Masque can stand erect and steady without bulwarks or
buttresses; but the music's meaning as a work of art is
dimmed at the least—lost altogether, I personally feel—
without the interplay of the minds of the first company.

How close was the association of those minds in interplay
can be understood from the admirable analysis by Mr Frank
Howes in the "Musical Pilgrim Series."[1] Side by side
therein are printed the first scenario by Dr Keynes and the
final interpretation of it for musical expression by Dr
Vaughan Williams, who wrote, in the printed score:

> The following synopsis and the more detailed scenario printed with
> the music differ in some particulars from the original scheme of the
> authors. For these alterations the composer alone is responsible.

Those "some particulars" are illuminating not only of the
whole artistic creation that is the Masque for Dancing, *Job*:
they also throw a brilliant light upon the wide creative
processes of musical composition, and in particular on those
of this Englishman *per se*.

Musically, too, *Job*'s score is a synthesis, a musical com-
bining of the various Vaughan Williamses we have met
during the years and (I hope) in these pages. The artistic
result is a unity, derived from the other unities of his
co-workers: a collective unity which only one mind could
create, as an integral offering to the gathered whole. For
example, is there another composer living who could,
without a trace of self-consciousness, write both a *Saraband
of the Sons of God* and a *Galliard of the Sons of the Morning*,
inventing, for each, music of suitable power and dignity?
The informing mind of Blake inspired Vaughan Williams
then, and his helpers (the orchestra included) directed his
mystically soaring mind into the practical business of the

[1] *The Dramatic Works of Vaughan Williams* (Oxford University Press, 1937).

visual stage where men and women must use their legs to dance. Everything we have tried to discover in Vaughan Williams in this study of his mind is to be found here—drama, in the acute characterization, for example; and the horror of Satan which appears in more developed shape in the F minor Symphony. Folk-song, too—there is no direct quotation, but in the dance of Job's six sons and three daughters the direction is given that "the figures of this dance should take suggestions from the dances 'Jenny pluck pears' and 'Hunsdon House.'" The music throughout is enlightened by an older English culture, by the Act-tunes of Purcell no less than by the stately dances that came earlier. The dignity of the ancient English Church surrounds us in the theatre. Here is Englishry indeed—a distillation of a complex race into one phial. The music flies back from Blake, poises above us, and comes to ground, with all its English blazons, in Rosebery Avenue.

For *Job* is a piece of to-day. The scale is enormous, the orchestral demands extensive, with triple wood-wind, tuba as well as three trombones, two harps, and organ. The added E-flat saxophone is used for a satirical picture of the bleating of Job's comforters. If ever old and new, tradition and modernity, past and future, were blended together, fused by creative power into a freshly grown element, we shall find all of them musically in *Job*.

Of the music Vaughan Williams has written for films there is little to say. For the most part scores are not available for study; and if they were, so closely is the musical pattern of 'movie' compositions forced to follow the timing of the frames that one would need the celluloid reels themselves and a 'run-through studio' to understand the good or bad, the invention or the padding, that the music contains. It was bibliographically a memorable moment when Vaughan Williams entered Denham Studios, score in hand, at the age of seventy; and the 'play-through' was done on a cracked and out-of-tune piano. The first tune—across the 'credits'—of 49*th Parallel* was splendid, and I am glad to record that this tune is available in print to all under the guise of *The New Commonwealth*, with admirable words by Harold Child. Some of the music for *Coastal Command* and also of *Scott of the Antarctic* has been recorded. For myself, I am incapable of judging film music without extra-musical information. Of Vaughan Williams's technical skill there could be no longer any doubt. One could, perhaps, wish that operatic opportunity had come to him at an earlier period in his development. I write those words without regret, and in full gratitude for what he has so generously given us.

Miscellany of Vocal Writings

THE influence of Vaughan Williams on English
Church music as practised to-day is to be felt in its
widest range and deepest musical value among the congregation and those who help them to join in hymn-singing.
Those editorial fingers, choosing this melody from ancient
store, rejecting that other which is unworthily retained
through associations of childhood, adapting a third—a folk-
tune, perhaps—to ritual use, have touched hands with many
millions of worshippers in the near half-century since the
first issue of *The English Hymnal*. The colonizing of far
wider territories was the aim of *Songs of Praise*, and the
scholarly but practical revival of true tradition that of *The
Oxford Book of Carols*. From the beginning he was aware (as
he says in his 1906 Preface on "The Music") that here was
"a moral rather than a musical issue."

> No doubt it requires a certain effort to tune oneself to the moral
> atmosphere implied by a fine melody; and it is far easier to dwell in
> the miasma of the languishing and sentimental hymn-tunes which
> often disfigure our services. Such poverty of heart may not be
> uncommon, but at least it should not be encouraged by those who
> direct the Services of the Church; it ought no longer to be true
> anywhere that the most exalted moments of a churchgoer's week
> are associated with music that would not be tolerated in any place
> of secular entertainment.

Out of the strength of his own heart and mind Vaughan
Williams, through those who gave him his projective
opportunity, erected anew the high monumental standard
of past ages. He added to his editorial labours the practical

example of a living composer; he enriched the hymnology with splendid, simple tunes of his own.

Though in liturgical music (including anthems) his contribution is slighter and somewhat scanty, Vaughan Williams has raised in this soil one mighty tree; the Mass in G minor, with the sapling that sprang from it, *O vos omnes*. In more than one way the Mass marks a climax of a period: a peak, if not an Everest. The late Sir Richard Terry had created at Westminster Cathedral during the years he directed the music there from 1901 an entirely new tradition of Roman Catholic liturgical music. Much of this tradition was rooted in a remote past that had been allowed to wither. Terry's achievement was that he daily and weekly gave full aural life to music which for three hundred years or so had slept on dusty shelves in libraries, material perhaps for antiquarians and scholars, but, most of it, unknown even to them. Terry's burning vitality, however, was not content even with the large quantity of music provided by the composers of the Golden Age. He sought out and encouraged living composers to write *a capella* works for his choir to sing in the regular offices. Stanford, Wood, Rootham, Lloyd, Buck, Holst, Bax, Howells, Oldroyd, and others wrote music for him, all of it sung by Terry's ardent and indefatigable band of choristers. But, we read in his biography,

> when Vaughan Williams first sent the Mass to him for comment, Terry wrote back: "I'm quite sincere when I say that it is the work one has all along been waiting for. In your individual and modern idiom you have really captured the old liturgical spirit and atmosphere."[1]

That was in 1922, and in 1924 Terry left the Cathedral.

The only work written by the composer in a direct re-creation of the polyphonic style of the earlier English masters (save for the adjacent motet), the Mass in G minor sums up in a curiously complete way that deeply mystical phase which his mind was going through immediately after the 1918 Armistice. In itself, as a composition, it is a full

[1] *Westminster Retrospect*, by Hilda Andrews (Oxford University Press, 1948).

and rounded expression of the mind. No single liturgical work, however, could contain all the thoughts, in all their phases and manifestations and developments, that must have crowded in on that mind at the 1922 period and before. Thus the remote and personal *Pastoral Symphony* was written simultaneously with the Mass; the Symphony, though utterly different in form and more pantheistic in outlook, is hardly less religious in feeling. *Flos Campi* and *Sancta Civitas* followed but a year or two later (1925–26). Nor is there any lack of mystical exaltation in the "Pastoral Episode," also produced in 1922, *The Shepherds of the Delectable Mountains.*

The connexion between the Mass and the *Pastoral Symphony* is, I feel, important. The two works are un-Germanic, unlike Bach, who had, behind the veil of the mind, been an inspiration to the composer, as he has told us. Each is written in the English tongue—one of the English tongues, I should say. Yet there is a parallelism of contrapuntal design that cannot but remind one of Debussy, and lead back through him to Moussorgsky; it appears in the *Pastoral,* with its orchestral pattern, but it also appears in the vocal Mass. In other respects the Mass owes little to Debussy, though it could not have been written had not his and other forerunning nationalists' brains occurred in earlier history. The English language is rethought; the best of its living elements are combined anew in the modern formula of an English-speaking composer.

The oddest thing about this splendid reincarnation of the other world of sound is that it is not austere. Because he threw away the coloured harness of the orchestral steed, there was a general critical tendency to treat the composer of the Mass as if he were an itinerant friar wearing a hair shirt. In fact, the music sounds lovely in the ear, the false relations are carefully planned to give richness of sound. In aural reception, the Mass is vibrant and not severe. It is also (I am told) delightful to sing—for the right singers! But is not that true of Byrd's Masses? Was he in reality so austere? I have never believed in the post-Ruskin legend of the grey purity of Gothic. Those giant-minded builders of our cathedrals had, I am sure, as well as a sense of line a vigorous sense of colour. The Mass is sensuous in sound, however architectural, in the Cathedral sense, it may be in outlines.

Prayer to the Father of Heaven should not be overlooked. It was written for the centenary of the birth of "my master, Hubert Parry, not as an attempt palely to reflect his incomparable art, but in the hope that he would have found in this work 'something characteristic.'" So runs Vaughan Williams's dedication. It is certainly 'characteristic,' though there is no other work in the list which can be mated with it as companion. It would appear (I have not heard it) to be effective, in the sense that the music is properly expressed in its own original style.

When we turn to the songs for solo voice and to the part-songs, one cycle rears up its head demanding immediate attention: *Merciles Beauty*, three rondels by Chaucer set for high voice (preferably soprano) with string trio. The publisher's date gives 1922. A consciously archaic work in the modal manner, this cycle has a curious penetration into one's inner memory. When I reread the score a day or two past I realized after a bar or two that I could recall its whole contents, especially the cunning of the artificer who could make our music of now fit without discomfort into the poet's verbal patterns. Unperformed to-day, it is a beautiful work, though I still think it wears the English chevron with a touch of self-consciousness.

As years have gone on the desire to write songs has, it seems, become dimmer in Vaughan Williams's mind. His lyrical music he has put into his operas, or into those glorious crystallizing tunes in which he can give us briefly the meaning of a whole symphonic movement. Some of the songs must, however, for a moment engage our attention.

Of *Linden Lea* I will say nothing but that it is a pity that its simple beauty has so long distracted singers' attention from equally good songs. The two settings, earlyish and latish respectively, of "Orpheus with his Lute" should be studied. The three Whitman songs are hard to make successful, but very vigorous; and of the Fredegond Shove poems Vaughan Williams made a great thing of "The New Ghost," and a less great, more reminiscent, and far more popular thing of "The Water Mill." Perhaps the best of the songs is "The Twilight People," to words by Seumas O'Sullivan—a folk-song, if ever there was one, but a folk-song written by a man of educated and experienced intellect.

The folk-song arrangements for piano with voice above are numerous and in most cases excellent—so musical, that is, as well as fitting. They cover years of thought and labour. Vaughan Williams paid generous tribute in an appendix to the life of Cecil Sharp to the excellence of the latter's piano accompaniments. Those of us who know a majority of the accompaniments written by both men (there was no rivalry) do not hesitate to choose the composer's, though it is likely that the collector's were more suitable to his work of the propagation of English song in the minds and throats of the ordinary people. No one can calculate the influence of either of these great propagators of the natural language of English music. Sharp, in a sense, begat Vaughan Williams. But I hazard an unstatistical guess that the latter has, in the end, done more than the former. To both be honour!

There are many part-songs and songs for schools and mixed companies in addition to those already treated in these pages. Few need separate mention here, but for personal reasons of preference I should like to single out one or two— *The New Commonwealth*, for example. The *Three Children's Songs* (to words by the Hon. Francis M. Farrer) are charming, especially when sung, as intended, by a choir of children. The Henley piece—*England, my England*—suffered a disaster on its first presentation (I will not recount the story); otherwise it might well have become a national song like Parry's *Jerusalem*. The rest of these vocal works I must offer to my readers in a sheaf, for him or her to accept as a harvest gathering, each to disentangle the wheat from the very few tares.

13

Epilogue

DOGGING my composer's footsteps, I have ventured to filch from his pocket, like a pupil of Fagin, his handkerchief of a title for my last movement. I shall not attempt to express in words that philosophic finality, that contrapuntal exegesis of ideas 'afore-stated,' of the great man. The maturity of a master is needed for clambering up such intellectual heights.

Yet in Vaughan Williams's music as a whole there cannot be found either finality or summary: neither in one work nor in all. The stream of music flows through him, and will "wind somewhere safe to sea." The music stands, but it is not static. Always it leads us on, and my pen is conscious that it may continue to lead him so much farther on his pilgrimage as to make its words démodé—the creaking spars of a disused windmill.

To comprehend and digest the whole of the fare which Vaughan Williams has spread out before us on his long table needs a hungry maw and a keen appetite. No queasy, querulous sticker-to-his-own-tastes will appreciate the variety of his provision. Yet every dish is nourishing: and if they are too many for one sitting, then there is to-morrow's breakfast, Tuesday's lunch, Thursday's dinner, and an exquisite extra supper on Saturday evening with, perhaps, the *Serenade to Music* as a nightcap.

"Through watches of the dark" music often pours across the mind of a man lying in bed, waiting for sleep. In the midnight reminiscent mood the feeble brain cannot, I find, always relate this jolly passage, or that engaging progression of chords, to any one particular work. With the

'classics,' the problem is easily solved, either by hard thought
or by reference to a score or two next morning; but with
romantics and contemporaries the sleepless dreamer has
merely the pleasurable irritation of memory without the
satisfaction of exact identity. I think, at this moment, of
Milhaud, Hindemith, and Szymanovsky, of Villa Lobos,
Prokofiev, and Medtner—not to mention by name certain
English composers of our time, or the little-heard Mahler
and Bruckner and Reger from among the larger host: even
Wagner.

Much of the music of the composers I have mentioned
partakes of the quality of wallpaper. It is beautifully
patterned, in admirable design; but it is offered to us in
strips, curved around like a roller.

Critical tendency has often turned towards the idea that
Vaughan Williams is a 'wallpaper' composer—that his
works all contain such deep imprints of his digital idiom as to
be each one in truth a strip off the predecessor and successor.

I cannot agree. To comprehend this great man's mind
one needs the study of all his many facets of radiance. It
would be impossible stylistically to introduce one bar of
Riders to the Sea into *Sir John in Love*, or one bar of either
into *Job*. The *Magnificat* is as much a religious work for
voices as the *Five Mystical Songs* and the *Benedicite*; the
differences in the use of the medium do not need to be explained. *Flos Campi* and the hopeful Shelley songs do not
conflict but complement each other. The early *Tallis
Fantasia* is as English and as central as the more obvious
Thanksgiving for Victory of full age. And does one wish, at
this stage of the argument, to contrast "The Twilight
People" with the Fourth Symphony? I hold the pen
stationary, in my hand. The word "unique" dripped from
the inkpot on half a dozen occasions, for no music has
ever been written by another composer of similar parlance
with *Sancta Civitas* and the Symphonies, for example. But
it was better to exclude that exclusive term of oddity; it was
too often true.

If we are to comprise within our minds all the thoughts of Vaughan Williams, over his fifty-five years of musical creation, we shall need a sense of literature, a love of varied means of musical expression, a feeling for both the general and the particular—rare qualities in the merely musical man or even the enlightened reader.

Without difficulty this chapter could end with a list of what I have once or twice referred to as those works of art which are "central to his mind." Nor, with Vaughan Williams, would it be arduous to fill pages with memories of his music, of his character and his kindness and his persistence, of his genius and his limitations, in a kind of panegyric peroration. Such poetic ebullience would be both foolish in the author and unsuitable to the subject.

The works remain, for our study, our edification, our enjoyment; only through them can our lives be illuminated by the mind of that great man—Ralph Vaughan Williams, O.M.

"Who wants the English Composer?"

by Ralph Vaughan Williams

THE following article appeared in the *R.C.M. Magazine*, vol. ix, No. 1, dated "Christmas Term, 1912," and is reprinted here by kind permission of the author and the Director of the Royal College of Music. Not only has it the historical importance of having expressed a much-needed truth at a right but early moment; it has also considerable relevance to the present state of music in England.

> Come, Muse, migrate from Greece and Ionia,
> Cross out, please, those immensely over-paid accounts,
> That matter of Troy and Achilles' wrath, and Æneas', Odysseus'
> wanderings,
> Placard "Removed" and "To Let" on the rocks of your snowy Parnassus,
> Repeat at Jerusalem, place the notice high on Jaffa's gate and on Mount
> Moriah,
> The same on the walls of your German, French and Spanish castles, and
> Italian collections,
> For know a better, fresher, busier sphere, a wide untried domain awaits,
> demands you.
> WALT WHITMAN, "Song of the Exposition."

It is reported that the head of a famous publishing firm once said, "Why do you young Englishmen go on composing? Nobody wants you."

Is not this what we all feel in our secret souls at times? Nobody wants the young English composer; he is unappreciated at home and unknown abroad. And, indeed, the composer who is not wanted in England can hardly desire to be known abroad, for though his appeal should be in the long run universal, art, like charity, should begin at home. If it is to be of any value it must grow out of the very life of himself, the community in which he lives, the nation to which he belongs.

Is it perhaps this misunderstanding of the very essence of the vitality of any art which makes the English composer a drug in the market? We are too fond in England of looking on music as a matter of detached appreciation. The English amateur believes with Rossini that there are only two kinds of music—good and bad—and if he can afford it, he prefers to import, together with the best brands of cigars and champagne, the best brands of music also. The connexion between music and every-day life is entirely severed.

Now, in no other art except music is this connexion doubted. No one with any pretence to culture would fail to keep abreast with all that his fellow-countrymen were saying in literature, painting, or drama. Such a man may well say, "I think Velasquez a greater painter than Augustus John, Goethe a greater poet than Masefield, and Dostoievsky a greater novelist than Arnold Bennett," yet he would know that unless he had seen and read the pictures, poems, novels, or plays of his contemporaries, he would lose one of the surest means of realizing what he himself was dimly and inarticulately feeling and thinking, and that the temper of the age was in danger of passing over him, leaving him untouched and unready.

And yet music, the subtlest, most sensitive, and purest means of self-expression, is supposed to be on a plane by itself, a thing detached from its surroundings, a mere sensation to be enjoyed by the epicure. Thus it comes about that the cultured amateur says to the composer, "What have you to offer me better than the great Masters? I have my Bach, my Beethoven, my Brahms. They are enough to satisfy me; or can you show me more subtle harmonies than Debussy, more striking orchestral effects than Strauss? If not, why should I bore myself by listening to you or trying to play you?" And the amateur, judged by his own standard, is perfectly right. The English composer is not and for many generations will not be anything like so good as the great Masters, nor can he do such wonderful things as Strauss and Debussy. But is he for this reason of no value to the community? Is it not possible that he has something to say to his own countrymen that no one of any other age and any other country can say? When English people realize this—that the composer is their own voice speaking through his art those things which they can only dimly grope for—then indeed the English composer will be wanted, if only he is ready.

But is the English composer ready? Does he keep his part of the bargain? The composer on his side is much too apt to look on his art from an aloof and detached point of view, to think of composition as a series of clever tricks which can be learnt and imitated. The desire to "do it too" whenever the newest thing comes over from abroad is very strong with us all. So long then as our composers are content to write operas which only equal Wagner in length, symphonies made up of scraps of Brahms at his dullest, or pianoforte pieces which are merely crumbs from Debussy's table, we can hardly blame the amateur for preferring the genuine article to the shoddy imitation.

We English composers are always saying, "Here are Wagner, Brahms, Grieg, Tchaikovsky, what fine fellows they are, let us try and do something like this at home," quite forgetting that the result will not sound at all like "this" when transplanted from its natural soil. It is all very well to catch at the prophet's robe, but the mantle of Elijah is apt, like all second-hand clothing, to prove the worst of misfits. We must be our own tailors, we must cut out for ourselves, try on for ourselves, and finally wear our own home-made garments, which, even if they are homely and home-spun, will at all events fit our bodies and keep them warm; otherwise, if we pick about among great ideas of foreign comopsers and try to cover our own nakedness with them, we are in danger of being the musical counterparts of the savage clothed in nothing but a top-hat and a string of beads.

How is the composer to find himself? How is he to stimulate his imagination in a way which will lead to his voicing the sentiments of himself and his fellows? I need hardly at this time of day point to the folk-song as a worthy study to all musicians, the germ from which all musical developments ultimately spring. But are there not other incentives for inspiration, imperfect perhaps and overlaid with dross, but pregnant with meaning to those who have ears to hear? Must not any genuine and unforced musical expression be full of suggestion to the musical inventor?

Our composers are much too fond of going to concerts. There they hear the finished product; what the artist should be concerned with is the raw material. Have not we all about us forms of musical expression which we can take and purify and raise to the level of great art? For instance, the lilt of the chorus at a music-hall joining in a popular song, the children dancing to a barrel organ, the rousing fervour of a Salvation Army hymn, St Paul's and a great choir singing in one of its festivals, the Welshmen striking up one of their own hymns whenever they win a goal at the international football match, the cries of the street pedlars, the factory girls singing their sentimental songs? Have all these nothing to say to us? Have we not in England occasions crying out for music? Do not all our great pageants of human beings, whether they take the form of a coronation or a syndicalist demonstration, require music for their full expression? We must cultivate a sense of musical citizenship; why should not the musician be the servant of the State and build national monuments like the painter, the writer, or the architect?

Art for art's sake has never flourished in England. We are often called inartistic because our art is unconscious. Our drama and poetry, like our laws and our constitution, have evolved by accident while we thought we were doing something else, and so it will be with music. The composer must not shut himself up and think about art, he must live with his fellows and make his art an expression of the whole life of the community—if we seek for art we shall not find it.

Modern music is in a state of ferment. Composers all the world over are trying new paths, new experiments. This you may say will not produce great composers: perhaps not at first. There are hardly any great composers, but there can be many sincere composers. There is nothing in the world worse than sham good music. There is no form of insincerity more subtle than that which is coupled with great earnestness of purpose and determination to do only the best and the highest—this unconscious insincerity which leads us to build up great designs which we cannot fill and to simulate emotions which we can only feel vicariously.

If we look back into the history of music we find a state of things almost exactly parallel to that of our own times: the musical revolution of the seventeenth century. Here we have the same ferment, the same striking out of new paths and new experiments. Here also we find an absence of great names. But this ferment, this age of experiments, made possible in time the advent of Johann Sebastian Bach. It was not his musical ancestry only that made it possible for Bach to be a great composer; the social conditions which immediately preceded him are also partly responsible for him. He was the last of a race of musicians who started humbly enough, but gradually rose to occupy the very highest musical posts amongst their fellow-townsmen. It was the sense of musical citizenship which produced them; they served the community as composers, as organists, as "town pipers," and it was out of this musical environment that there came at last the greatest of all musicians.

Perhaps the future has another Bach in store for us and perhaps he will be an Englishman, but if that is to be so we must prepare the way for him.

A Brief Chronology of Vaughan Williams's
Main Extant Compositions[1]

1903.
    Willow Wood (chorus, soloist, and orchestra).
    The House of Life (song-cycle).

1905.
    Toward the Unknown Region (women's chorus and orchestra).

1906.
    First Norfolk Rhapsody.

1909.
    The Wasps (orchestra).
    On Wenlock Edge (song-cycle with piano quintet).
    Fantasia on a Theme by Thomas Tallis (strings).

1910.

(*c.* 1905–10).
    A Sea Symphony (chorus, soloists, and orchestra).

1911.
    Five Mystical Songs (song-cycle, voice, chorus, and orchestra).

1911–14.
    Hugh the Drover (opera) (performed 1924).

1912.
    Fantasia on Christmas Carols (soloist, chorus, and orchestra).

1913.
    Five English Folk-songs (freely arranged for S.A.T.B.).

1914.
    A London Symphony (revised 1920).
    The Lark Ascending (violin and orchestra) (performed 1921).

1920.
    Four Hymns (voice and orchestra).

1922.
    A Pastoral Symphony.
    Mass in G minor (chorus).
    The Shepherds of the Delectable Mountains (opera).

---

[1] See List of Works for further particulars.

1925. *Flos Campi* (viola, chorus, and orchestra).
       Concerto Accademico (violin and strings).

1926. *Sancta Civitas* (chorus, soloists, and orchestra).

1929. *Sir John in Love* (opera).

1930. *Benedicite* (chorus, soloist, and orchestra).
       Job (masque for dancing).

1932. *Magnificat* (chorus, soloist, and orchestra).

1934. Piano Concerto (also rewritten for two pianos and
       orchestra, 1946).
       Viola Suite.

1935. Symphony in F minor.

1936. *The Poisoned Kiss* (opera).
       Dona Nobis Pacem (chorus, soloists, and orchestra).
       Five Tudor Portraits (chorus, soloists, and orchestra).

1937. *Flourish for a Coronation* (soloists and orchestra).
       Riders to the Sea (opera).

1938. *Serenade to Music* (soloists and orchestra).

1939. *Five Variants of "Dives and Lazarus"* (strings).

1940. *"Six Choral Songs* to be sung in time of war"
       (unison chorus and orchestra).

1942. *Household Music* (string quartet).

1943. Symphony in D major.

1944. Oboe Concerto (strings).

1945. Quartet No. 2 in A minor (with viola lead).

(1944–47) 1948. Symphony in E minor.

A List of Works

THIS List of Works will be, it is hoped, as complete as possible at the date when this book goes finally to press: complete, that is, as regards items extant. More details, and a different arrangement of order, will be found in the bibliography made by the author for Grove's *Dictionary of Music and Musicians*, which, edited by Mr Eric Blom, is in preparation for its fifth edition. This plainer, less meticulous 'list' will better suit this book.

Though a semblance of date order is shown, no exactitude is sought; for, as the composer himself wrote in 1949, "I fear I cannot help you at all over dates of composition—it often spread over years." The date column may be thought of broadly as showing composition, performance, or publication. Historically this general treatment is not as inaccurate as it may appear; and greater detail is to be available, as said above, in the new *Grove*. None of the many arrangements is specifically listed. Works "scrapped" (in the composer's word) are also omitted. The method used under works for chorus or orchestra is to show the exceptionals, the ordinaries being assumed from the title of the section.

The result, a compromise, is at the same time illuminating.

INSTRUMENTAL WORKS

(a) For Orchestra

Symphonic Impression: *In the Fen Country* (1904) (rev. 1905 and 1907. Orchn. rev. 1935).
Three Norfolk Rhapsodies: No. 1, in E minor (1906).
Fantasia on a Theme by Thomas Tallis (for strings) (1909).
Overture to *The Wasps* (Aristophanes) (1909).
A London Symphony (1914) (rev. 1920).
A Pastoral Symphony (1922).
Job (a masque for dancing) (1930).
Prelude and Fugue in C minor (1930).
The Running Set (founded on Traditional Dance Tunes) (1935).

Symphony in F minor (1935).
Five Variants of "Dives and Lazarus" (1939).
Fantasia on "Greensleeves."
Symphony, D major (1943).
Symphony, E minor (1944–47).
Partita for Double String Orchestra (1948).

(*b*) For Solo Instruments with Orchestra

The Lark Ascending (romance for violin and orchestra on a poem by George Meredith) (1914) (performed 1921).
Violin Concerto in D minor (strings) (originally called *Concerto Accademico*) (1925).
Concerto for Pianoforte and Orchestra[1] (1934).
Suite for Viola and Orchestra (in three groups) (1934).
Concerto for Oboe and Strings (1944).
Concerto for Two Pianofortes and Orchestra[1] (arranged from the above) (1946).

(*c*) Chamber Music

String Quartet in G minor (1908) (rev. 1921).
Fantasy Quintet (2 violins, 2 violas, 'cello) (*c.* 1910).
Six Studies in English Folk-song ('cello and piano, and arrangements) (1927).
Household Music: Three Preludes on Welsh Hymn-tunes (string quartet or other available instruments) (1942).
String Quartet in A minor (1945).

(*d*) Pianoforte Solo

Canon and Two-part Invention.
Two Two-part Inventions.

[1] The Pianoforte Concerto is available, for purposes of study and practice, in a version for two pianos made by Vally Lasker; but it must be clearly understood that in that reduction one piano part is that of the soloist in the original one-piano work, and the second piano part is a transcription of the original orchestral part.

Valse lente and *Nocturne*.
Hymn-tune Prelude (on Gibbons's *Song* 13).
Suite of Six Short Pieces (arrd. as *Charterhouse Suite* for strings).
The Lake in the Mountains (from the film music for *Forty-ninth Parallel*).

(e) FOR TWO PIANOFORTES

Introduction and Fugue (1946).

(f) FOR ORGAN SOLO

Three Preludes on Welsh Hymn-tunes (1920).
Preludes and Fugue in C minor (1930).

VOCAL WORKS

(a) FOR CHORUS AND ORCHESTRA

Toward the Unknown Region (Walt Whitman) (1905) (rev. 1918).
Willow Wood (women's chorus and baritone solo) (Dante Gabriel Rossetti) (1903) (performed 1909).
A Sea Symphony (soprano and baritone, chorus and orchestra) (Walt Whitman) (*c.* 1905–10).
Five Mystical Songs (baritone) (George Herbert) (1911).
Fantasia on Christmas Carols (baritone) (1912).
Flos Campi (viola solo, small chorus, and small orchestra) (wordless chorus, with mottoes from *The Song of Solomon*) (1925).
Sancta Civitas (tenor, baritone, semi-chorus, etc.) (The Bible) (1926).
Benedicite (soprano) (*The Song of the Three Holy Children* and J. Austin) (1930).
Three Choral Hymns (Miles Coverdale) (1930).
The Hundredth Psalm (Prayer Book) (1930).
In Windsor Forest (cantata adapted from *Sir John in Love*) (see "Music for the Stage") (1931).
Magnificat (soprano, women's chorus, and flute) (1932).

Dona Nobis Pacem (soprano and baritone) (Whitman and sacred texts) (1936).

Five Tudor Portraits (contralto and baritone) (Skelton) (1936).

Flourish for a Coronation (The Bible, Chaucer, and others) (1937).

"Nothing is here for tears" (unison) (from Milton).

"*Six Choral Songs* to be sung in time of War" (unison) (Shelley) (1940).

Thanksgiving for Victory (soprano and speaker) (The Bible, Shakespeare, and Kipling) (1945).

"Folk-songs of the Four Seasons" (women's voices) (1950).

(b) For Solo Voices and Orchestra

Four Hymns (tenor, viola, and strings) (Jeremy Taylor, Isaac Watts, Richard Crashaw, Robert Bridges) (1920).

Serenade to Music (sixteen soloists) (Shakespeare) (1938).

(c) For Unaccompanied Chorus

Three Elizabethan Part-songs (Shakespeare and Herbert) (S.A.T.B.) (*c.* 1891–96).

"Sound Sleep" (Christina Rossetti) (S.S.A. acc.) (1903).

"Down among the dead men" (T.T.B.B.) (1908).

Eleven English Folk-songs (unison acc.) (1910).

"Rest" and "Ring out, ye bells" (Christina Rossetti and Sidney) (S.S.A.T.B.).

"Old Folks at Home" (Foster) (T.T.B.B.) (*c.* 1908).

Five English Folk-songs (S.A.T.B.) (1913).

"Love is a Sickness" (S. Daniel) (ballet for 4 voices) (1918).

"Where is home for me?" (Gilbert Murray, after Euripides) (2 pts. and pianoforte) (1922).

Dirge for Fidele (Shakespeare) (2 pts. and pianoforte) (1922).

"Come away, Death" (Shakespeare) (S.S.A.T.B.).

"It was a lover" (Shakespeare) (2 pts. and pianoforte).

"Ca' the Yowes" (tenor and S.A.T.B.) (1922).

"Let us now praise famous men" (Ecclesiasticus) (unison acc.) (1923).

"The Seeds of Love" (T.T.B.B.) (1923).

"The Turtle Dove" (baritone and S.A.T.B.) (1924).

Three Children's Songs for a Spring Festival (Frances M. Farrer) (unison acc.) (1930).
"An Acre of Land (T.T.B.B. and other arrts.) (1934).
Nine Carols (T.T.B.B.).
"The Ploughman," "The World it went well with me then" (T.T.B.B.).
"I'll never love thee more" (S.A.T.B.).
"Darest thou now, O Soul?" (unison acc.).
"John Dory" (S.A.T.B.).
"Mannin Veen" (Manx) (S.A.T.B.) (1939).
"The New Commonwealth" (Harold Child) (unison and various arrts.) (from *Forty-ninth Parallel*—see "Film Music") (1943).
"England, my England" (Henley) (unison and other arrts., acc.) (1941).
"Valiant-for-Truth" (motet) (Bunyan) (S.A.T.B.) .
(A number of other folk-song arrangements in the *Motherland Song Book* and elsewhere).

(*d*) FOR SOLO VOICE (MOSTLY WITH PIANO ACCOMPANIMENT)

"Whither must I wander?" (R. L. Stevenson) (*c.* 1894).
"How can the tree but wither?" (Lord Vaux) (*c.* 1896).
"The splendour falls" (Tennyson) (*c.* 1896).
"Claribel" (Tennyson) (*c.* 1896).
"Dreamland" (Christina Rossetti) (*c.* 1898).
"Linden Lea" (W. Barnes) (*c.* 1900).
"Blackmwore by the Stour" (W. Barnes) (*c.* 1900).
"The Winter's Willow" (W. Barnes) (*c.* 1903).
"Tears, idle tears" (Tennyson) (before 1903).
"When I am dead" (Christina Rossetti) (before 1903).
"Orpheus with his lute" (first setting) (Shakespeare) (before 1903).
The House of Life (a cycle of six sonnets) (Dante Gabriel Rossetti) (1903).
"Cradle Song" (Coleridge) (*c.* 1905).
Songs of Travel—I (R. L. Stevenson) (before 1905).
Songs of Travel—II (R. L. Stevenson) (before 1907).
"Boy Johnny," and "If I were queen" (Christina Rossetti).
"L'Amour de moy" (arr.) (before 1907).
"Buonaparte" (Hardy) (before 1909).
"The Sky above the roof" (Mabel Dearmer) (*c.* 1909).

On Wenlock Edge (song cycle) (A. E. Housman) (tenor, piano quintet) (1909).
Folk-songs from Sussex (from the Merrick collection).
Folk-songs from the Eastern Counties.
Five Mystical Songs (George Herbert) (1911). (Also under "Choral Works.")
Merciles Beauty (Chaucer) (string trio) (1922).
Three Poems (Walt Whitman) (1925).
Four Poems (Fredegond Shove) (1925).
Two Poems (Seumas O'Sullivan) (unacc. *ad lib.*) (1925).
"Orpheus with his lute" (second setting) (Shakespeare).
"Take, O take those lips away" (Shakespeare).
"When icicles hang by the wall" (Shakespeare).
"She's like the swallow" (Newfoundland folk-song) (1934).
"Greensleeves" (traditional, adapted from *Sir John in Love*).
Six English Folk-songs (arr.) (1935).
Two English Folk-songs (voice and violin).
Two French Folk-songs (1937).
Two Old German Songs.
Nine Housman Songs (voice and violin) (MS.).
> (Various songs separately issued from the operas *Hugh the Drover* and *Sir John in Love*.)

(e) CHURCH MUSIC

Three Motets: "O praise the Lord" (triple chorus unacc.); "O clap your hands" (double chorus, brass, and organ); "Lord, Thou has been our refuge" (chorus, semi-chorus, and orchestra) (*c.* 1913).
Mass in G minor (unacc.) (*c.* 1922).
"O vos omnes" (unacc.) (1922).
Festival *Te Deum* (on traditional tunes) (S.A.T.B., and organ) (1928).
The Airmen's Hymn (unison).
"All hail the power" (tune—*Miles Lane*) (S.A.T.B.)
Services in D Minor (for the complete day, Matins, Communion, and Evensong) (unison, S.A.T.B., and organ).
"A Hymn of Freedom."
"My soul, praise the Lord."
"O, how amiable" (S.A.T.B., and organ) (1934).

O

Holy Communion (traditional setting).

Te Deum in G major (S.A.T.B., and organ) (1937).

"The Souls of the Righteous" (treble, tenor, and bass, with unacc. S.A.T.B.) (1947).

"The Voice out of the Whirlwind" (S.A.T.B., and organ) (1947).

"Prayer to the Father of Heaven" (S.A.T.B. unacc.) (1948).

(f) HYMN TUNES AND CAROLS

In *The English Hymnal:*
> E.H. 152: *Down Ampney* ("Come down, O Love divine").
> 273: *Magda* ("Saviour, again to thy dear name").
> 368: *King's Weston* ("At the name of Jesus").
> 524: *Randolph* ("God be with you till we meet again").
> 541: *White Gates* ("Fierce raged the tempest o'er the deep").
> 624: *Salve Festa Dies* ("Hail thee, Festival Day!").
> 641: *Sine Nomine* ("For all the Saints").
> Also a number of arrangements of English traditional melodies and other early hymn-tunes, mostly unacknowledged.

In *Songs of Praise* (enlarged edition):
> S.P. 58: *Oakley* ("The night is come like to the day").
> 126: *Mantegna* ("Into the woods my master went").
> 213: *Cumnor* ("Servants of God, or sons").
> 302: *Marathon* ("Servants of the great adventure").
> 316: *Guildford* ("England arise! the long, long night is over").
> 319: *Abinger* ("I vow to thee, my country").
> 432: *Famous Men* (canticle) ("Let us now praise famous men").
> Also three descants (to S.P. 65 "Helmsley," 87 "Cruger," and 437 "Eventide") as well as arrangements mostly unacknowledged.

In *The Oxford Book of Carols:*
> O.B.C. 173: *The Golden Carol.*
> 185: *Wither's Rocking Hymn.*
> 186: *Snow in the Street.*
> 196: *Blake's Cradle Song.*

CAROLS

Eight Traditional English Carols.
Twelve Traditional Carols from Herefordshire.

MUSIC FOR THE STAGE

(a) OPERAS

The Shepherds of the Delectable Mountains ('pastoral episode' adapted from Bunyan's *The Pilgrim's Progress* (included later in *The Pilgrim's Progress—see* below)) (1922).
The Wasps (Aristophanes) (overture and incidental music) (1909).
Hugh the Drover (ballad opera, with Harold Child) (1911–14).
Sir John in Love (Shakespeare's *Merry Wives of Windsor*) (1929).
The Poisoned Kiss, or The Empress and the Necromancer (romantic extravaganza) (Evelyn Sharp) (1936).
Riders to the Sea (J. M. Synge) (1937).
The Pilgrim's Progress (a morality founded on Bunyan's allegory of the same name) (1948–49).

(b) BALLETS

Old King Cole (1923).
On Christmas Night (a quodlibet on the story adapted from Dickens's *A Christmas Carol*) (1926).
Job (a masque for dancing founded on William Blake's illustrations for *The Book of Job* by Geoffrey Keynes and Gwendolen Raverat) (1930–33).
The Bridal Day (masque for dancing, founded on Spenser's *Epithalamion* by Ursula Wood) (MS).

(c) FILM MUSIC

Forty-ninth Parallel (1940–41).
Coastal Command (1942).
The People's Land (1943).
The Story of a Flemish Farm (1943).
Stricken Peninsula (1945).
The Loves of Joanna Godden (1947).
Scott of the Antarctic (1948–49).

BOOKS WRITTEN OR EDITED

Purcell, "Welcome Odes" (Purcell Society's Edition) (1904–6).
The English Hymnal (editor of music) (1906).
Songs of Praise (with Percy Dearmer and Martin Shaw) (1925).
The Oxford Book of Carols (with Percy Dearmer and Martin Shaw) (1928).
"English Folk-song" (pamphlet written for the English Folk Dance and Song Society).
National Music (1934).
Bach's B minor Mass adapted for the English Liturgy (not for sale) (1940–45).

Index

The index is divided into two parts. The first contains the names of people mentioned in the text, with here and there an entry of a page which gives not the writer's name but only a work of his. The second contains a list of references to the works written and edited by Ralph Vaughan Williams mentioned in the text. The songs and the symphonies are grouped. All references to Biblical writers and books are given under "Bible."

INDEX NOMINUM

213

INDEX OPERUM

Five mystical songs 106 + p. 99–100; 206; 83 103, –6

See also Herbert

On Wenlock Edge – v. Housman refs